AMAZIN   ES

200 EXTRAORDINARY DESTINATIONS

THE SUNDAY TIMES

magazine

Published by Times Books
An imprint of HarperCollins *Publishers*
Westerhill Road
Bishopbriggs
Glasgow G64 2QT
times.books@harpercollins.co.uk
www.harpercollins.co.uk

Paperback edition 2019

© Times Newspapers Ltd 2019

A catalogue record for this book
is available from the British Library.

ISBN 978-0-00-833414-7

10 9 8 7 6 5 4 3 2 1

Printed in Slovenia

Editors: Ed Grenby and Katie Bowman

Picture editor: Kate Hockenhull

Designer: Dave Rice

Writers: Amanda Hyde, Jeremy Lazell,
Alex Allen, Lucy Thackray, Alicia Miller,
Liz Edwards and Nick Redman

Additional writers: Susan d'Arcy, Nikki Bayley,
Leo Bear, Annie Bennett, Tom Bennett, Katie
Bowman, Anna Brooke, Emma Broomfield,
Jon Burbage, Alicia Burrell, Gemma Champ,
Lee Cobaj, Linda Cookson, Hannah Coussé,
Valerio Esposito, Lauren Everitt, Alex Flood,
Sarah Gibbons, Laura Goodman, Laura
Goulden, Ed Grenby, Clementine Hain-Cole,
Chris Haslam, Jeremy Head, Ellen Himelfarb,
Tamara Hinson, Alessia Horwich, Sally
Howard, Fiona Kerr, Kate Leahy, Jamie
Lafferty, Rod MacKenzie, Robin McKelvie,
Richard Mellor, Kankshi Mehta, Rebecca
Milner, Sean Newsom, Mary Novakovich,
Helen Ochyra, Joanne O'Connor, Tim Phedon,
Hannah Ralph, Tamzin Reynolds,
Alex Robinson, Mark Smith, Rachel Spence,
Stanley Stewart, Matthew Teller, Annabelle
Thorpe, Adrian Tierney-Jones, Nigel Tisdall,
Nina Zietman.

For the publishers: Elizabeth Donald, Dylan
Hamilton, Jethro Lennox, Keith Moore and
Kevin Robbins.

The Sunday Times Travel Magazine was
first published in 2003, and since then the
monthly glossy has established itself as
Britain's best-selling holiday title.
It is available at all good newsagents and
supermarkets in the UK, and leading stores
around the world, as well as by subscription:
call 01293 312214 in the UK, or visit
sundaytimestravel.co.uk.

Introduction

I locked them in a room. I took away the mini-bar, I took away their spa privileges, and — when even that didn't break them — I parental-controlled the TV so it could show only the Bloomberg Business Channel. Then I simply left them, *The Sunday Times Travel Magazine*'s finest minds, to discuss, argue, arm wrestle or do whatever it took to whittle down the list of 850 amazing places on our shortlist to just the 200 *most* amazing.

It took blood, sweat, tears and hundreds of those little tubs of UHT milk, but in the end we got there. And then the hard work started.

Because we're a glossy magazine, we've scoured the planet, and our photographers' portfolios, to match all our choices with the spectacular imagery that is our stock in trade.

And because we never feel like we've done our jobs properly unless we're giving readers some sneaky inside-track advice that they won't get from brochures or guidebooks or websites or tourist boards, we've accompanied each entry with a won't-read-it-anywhere-else tip from one of our expert editors.

That, I hope, will make this book a boon for both armchair adventurers and those who are actively planning their next trip. Sadly, all the coffee-creamer-fuelled arguments in the world couldn't make room for the level of detail we'd like to have included; but for that you can subscribe to the magazine at sundaytimestravel.co.uk, and get 164 pages of inspiration and in-depth information delivered to your door every month.

Meanwhile, I hope you enjoy *Amazing Places*. Just not that much. The idea is to put the book down and get out there, too...

Ed Grenby
Editor, *The Sunday Times Travel Magazine*

Amazing Places

8 **Monument Valley, USA**
10 Sveti Stefan, Montenegro
11 Costa Rica
12 **The Bund, Shanghai**
15 Piton Mountains, St Lucia
15 La Tomatina, Buñol, Spain
16 Charles Bridge, Prague
18 Shibden Valley, Calderdale,
    England
19 Carnival, Rio de Janeiro
20 Los Angeles, USA
22 **Whitsunday Islands, Australia**
25 Oktoberfest, Munich
25 Okavango, Botswana
25 The Bungle Bungles, Australia
26 Khao Phing Kan, Thailand
28 The Nile, Egypt
31 Las Teresitas, Tenerife
31 **Holi Festival, India**
32 Wormsloe Plantation,
    Georgia, USA
32 Kuala Lumpur, Malaysia
35 Amalfi Coast, Italy
35 Quiraing, Isle of Skye
35 Festival of the Sahara, Tunisia
36 Dubai, UAE
37 Samburu National Park, Kenya
38 **Neuschwanstein Castle, Bavaria,
    Germany**
40 Seventy Islands, Palau
40 The Treasury, Petra, Jordan
43 Moscow, Russia
44 **Tikal, Guatemala**
46 Richmond Park, England
49 Angkor Wat, Cambodia
49 Hawkdun Range, New Zealand
50 Keyhole Arch, California
50 Teahupoo, Tahiti
50 **Amsterdam**
52 Sossusvlei, Namib Desert, Namibia
55 Giant's Causeway,
    Northern Ireland
55 Damnoen Saduak Floating Market,
    Bangkok
57 Lion Rock, Hong Kong
58 The Maldives
59 Dubrovnik, Croatia
60 **Wat Muang, Thailand**
63 **Alkmaar tulip fields, Netherlands**
63 Pamukkale, Turkey
63 **Namolokama, Kaua'i, Hawaii**
65 Cape Town, South Africa

8 Monument Valley

12 Shanghai

22 Whitsunday Islands

31 Holi Festival

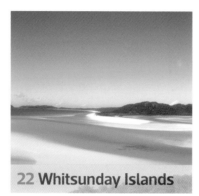

38 Germany

44 Guatemala

50 Amsterdam

60 Thailand

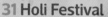

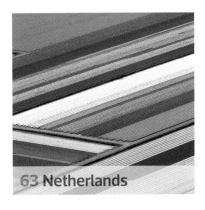

63 Netherlands

63 Hawaii

80 Rio

84 Kerala

88 Chicago

94 Samoa

101 Machu Picchu

117 Seattle

66 Songkran Water Festival, Thailand
66 Cape Verde
69 Arc de Triomphe, Paris
69 Lake Bogoria, Kenya
71 Svalbard, Norway
72 Zaanse Schans, Netherlands
74 The Glacier Express, Swiss Alps
74 Las Fallas Festival, Valencia, Spain
76 Derwent Fells, Lake District
79 Borneo, Asia
79 Sandy Spit, British Virgin Islands
80 **Rio de Janeiro, Brazil**
82 Santorini, Greece
83 Church of the Saviour on Blood, St Petersburg
84 **Kerala, India**
87 Tamba, Japan
88 **Chicago, USA**
88 Alsace, France
88 Chefchaouen, Morocco
91 Calabria, Italy
92 Berlin, Germany
94 **To-Sua Ocean Trench, Upolu, Samoa**
94 Empire State Building, New York
97 Lake Baikal, Russia
99 Vanuatu, South Pacific
99 West Lake, Hangzhou, China
99 Monti Sibillini National Park, Italy
101 **Machu Picchu, Peru**
102 Stockholm, Sweden
103 Pointe d'Esny, Mauritius
104 Steptoe Butte State Park, Washington, USA
104 St Mary, Jamaica
107 Singapore
108 Kakku Pagodas, Myanmar
111 Morondava, Madagascar
113 Steakhouse, Buenos Aires
113 Lac Blanc, Chamonix, France
115 El Nido, Philippines
117 **Seattle, USA**
117 **Port Quin Bay, Cornwall**
117 Ganesh Visarjan Festival, Mumbai
119 Hoher Kasten, Switzerland
121 Borobudur, Indonesia
121 Ponta Grossa, Ceará, Brazil
122 Havana, Cuba
123 Uluru, Australia
125 Bodiam Castle, East Sussex, UK
126 Oruro Carnival, Bolivia
126 Tunnel of Love, Ukraine
126 **South Beach, Miami**

128 Budapest, Hungary
130 Myrtos Beach, Kefallonia
132 Salzburg, Austria
132 Coimbra, Portugal
135 Eiffel Tower, Paris
135 Moon Hill, Yangshuo, China
136 Grenada, Caribbean
137 **Brussels, Belgium**
139 Hang En Cave, Vietnam
141 Pyhä Lake, Finland
141 The Cook Islands
141 **Serengeti National Park, Tanzania**
142 Procida, Italy
144 Seljalandsfoss, Iceland
144 Provence, France
146 Harbin Snow and Ice Festival, China
149 Brecon Beacons, Wales
149 Blue Hole, Belize
149 **San Francisco, USA**
150 Zakynthos, Greece
151 La Boca, Buenos Aires
153 **Antarctica**
154 Brighton Pier, East Sussex, UK
154 Praia da Concha, Portugal
156 Bazaruto Archipelago, Mozambique
158 Mount Fuji, Japan
159 Baja California, Mexico
161 **Istanbul, Turkey**
163 The Abacos, Bahamas
163 Yellowstone National Park, USA
163 The Himalayas
164 Longsheng, China
165 Marrakech, Morocco
166 Fly Geyser, Nevada, USA
169 Venice, Italy
171 Plitvice Lakes National Park, Croatia
173 Ranthambore National Park, India
173 Luskentyre Sands, Isle of Harris, UK
175 **Albi, France**
176 101 Tower, Taipei, Taiwan
177 Fiordland National Park, New Zealand
179 Bruges, Belgium
179 Aarhus, Denmark
179 **Easter Island, Chile**
180 London, England
181 Great Barrier Reef, Australia
182 Mount Bromo, Java
184 Chichén Itzá, Mexico
184 **Havasu Falls, Arizona, USA**
184 Sicily, Italy
187 Taj Mahal, India
188 Dead Sea, Middle East

117 Cornwall

126 Miami

137 Brussels

141 Serengeti

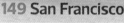
149 San Francisco

153 Antarctica

161 Istanbul

175 France

179 Easter Island

184 Arizona

200 Sydney

217 Albuquerque

218 Kyoto

226 Abu Dhabi

237 Bora Bora

248 Washington DC

189 Kirkjufell, Iceland
191 Etosha National Park, Namibia
192 Lake Waikopiro, New Zealand
192 Empty Quarter, Oman
192 Paro Taktsang, Bhutan
194 Manhattan, New York
196 Plaza de España, Seville
197 Quintana Roo, Mexico
198 Mosel River, Germany
198 Boudhanath Stupa, Kathmandu, Nepal
200 **Sydney Harbour Bridge**
202 Ditchling Beacon, South Downs, UK
202 Kandy, Sri Lanka
202 Abraham Lake, Alberta, Canada
205 Morris Island Lighthouse, South Carolina, USA
206 Colosseum, Rome
206 Geiranger Fjord, Norway
208 Canouan, St Vincent and the Grenadines
210 The Camargue, France
213 River Li, China
213 Faroe Islands
213 Frégate Island, Seychelles
214 Barcelona, Spain
217 **Albuquerque, New Mexico, USA**
218 **Fushimi Inari Taisha, Kyoto, Japan**
218 Taverna, Greece
220 Lake Pehoé, Patagonia, Chile
223 Algar de Benagil, Portugal
223 Olhuveli Island, Maldives
223 Prosecco Road, Treviso, Italy
225 Aït Benhaddou, Morocco
226 **Grand Mosque, Abu Dhabi, UAE**
226 Walt Disney World, Florida, USA
228 Salar de Uyuni, Bolivia
230 Blue Cypress Lake, Florida, USA
231 Florence, Italy
233 Great Wall, China
235 Logar Valley, Slovenia
235 Halnaker, West Sussex, UK
235 Burano, Venice
237 **Bora Bora, French Polynesia**
239 Grand Canyon, USA
241 Andalusia, Spain
241 Pura Ulun Danu Bratan, Bali, Indonesia
242 Ginza, Tokyo
244 Acropolis, Greece
245 Rajasthan, India
246 Giza, Egypt
248 **Washington DC, USA**
248 Orcia Valley, Tuscany, Italy
251 Buddha Park, Laos

Monument Valley, USA

As cinematically symbolic of the West as John Wayne's Stetson, Monument Valley's widescreen vistas make the ultimate movie set. (Hell, director John Ford was so taken with these sandstone soufflés across Utah and Arizona that he made nine of his films here, setting up his camera to shoot wagon trails towing dust clouds along the track seen here streaked with headlights.) But the scenery round this way doesn't need a script to deliver drama: at sunrise, these buttes materialise in a slow fade, silhouetted against a dip-dye sky that graduates from coral pink to petrol blue; and at sunset, they fade like the headstones of gods buried in the desert. Lights... camera...

Editor's tip: You can take your car through the looped valley road yourself for £15, though be aware that Monument Valley is not a US National Park — it's part of the Navajo Nation Reservation, so stick to the signposted tracks.

Sveti Stefan, Montenegro

There's a golden glow to this tiny island off Montenegro's coast — and it's not just down to the smattering of honey-hued buildings. Back in the 1960s, this 15th-century fishing village was transformed into a state-owned seaside refuge for the rich and famous, where guests including Liz Taylor, Sophia Loren and Princess Margaret partied far away from prying eyes. But when Yugoslavia crumbled, the hotel went with it, slowly decaying — until the swanky Aman hotel group reversed its fortunes in 2011. Now, mega-rich guests once again book into meticulously converted stone houses, trimmed in pink mimosa and trailing bougainvillea.

Editor's tip: You can't visit the island unless you're staying at the Aman resort (which costs upwards of £700 per night) — but Olive, the hotel-owned restaurant on the mainland, has this photo-worthy view from across the water.

Costa Rica

Take four per cent of the world's plant and animal species; shoehorn them into a country roughly half the size of England; then throw in volcanoes and beaches, cloud forests and jungles. *That's* Costa Rica, or 'rich coast', the most appropriately named country on Earth. And because Costa Rica is so small, even a 10-day trip is long enough for a satisfying bite of the best beaches and parks — with rafting, riding, canyoning and trekking for adventure addicts. No slumming it, either: Costa Rica was a pioneer of environmental tourism, and boutique eco-lodges abound.

Editor's tip: The one national park you mustn't miss is Tortuguero. Marooned at the northern tip of Costa Rica's Caribbean coast, this rainforest Eden shelters a crazy array of wildlife, including jaguars and tapirs, turtles and poison dart frogs.

The Bund, Shanghai

T'ai chi looks so calm and serene in the early-morning light — but don't get too close: it isn't called a martial art for nothing. These ladies are wielding fans with bamboo ribs that originally held sharp daggers at the ends; once snapped open, they became deadly weapons. Which would be pretty handy today, in an era where citizens have to fight for every square centimetre of personal space in this 24 million-strong mega-city. Even The Bund, Shanghai's iconic strip of spacious 1920s riverfront on the western bank of the Huangpu river, fills up fast. The draw? An eye-popping front-row vision of the world's future: across the river stands the space-age district of Pudong, an exotic forest of skyscrapers that looks its neon-lit best come nightfall. Centre stage is the Pearl Tower, a giant toy ray gun aimed at the smog-filled heavens. Set phasers to stun…

Editor's tip: To witness these t'ai chi-ers in action, you need to arrive at sunrise (see what time that is on timeanddate.com). You'll also see kite-fliers, runners, even ballroom dancers.

Piton Mountains, St Lucia

The Caribbean isn't short of selfie backdrops, but the Pitons are hard to beat. Dipping a toe in the ocean, St Lucia's iconic twin volcanic cones rise above a lush, hanging rainforest offering plenty of incentive to ditch the sunlounger for a day (aerial tram for the indolent; zip-lines and hiking trails for the active). St Lucia is an island of two halves — the north has golden beaches and great nightlife, the south has the stylish resorts (with that dramatic Piton backdrop), but mostly black volcanic sand. This means St Lucia cries out to be done as a two-centre holiday, with springtime (especially May) having the best weather and a cracking jazz festival.

Editor's tip: Friday night 'Jump Up' street party in Gros Islet (a fishing village towards the northern tip of St Lucia) is an institution. But arrive late — locals don't pitch up until 11pm.

La Tomatina, Buñol, Spain

It's the 'world's biggest food fight' — a squelchy, scarlet brawl in the sleepy Valencian town of Buñol, during which 20,000 people pelt each other with 160 tonnes of over-ripe tomatoes until the streets are paved with passata. Folklore suggests this bizarre festival started in the 1940s as an impromptu fight between unruly teens and locals on a parade. These days, there's an odd kind of order to the chaos : the pelting only begins once a ham has been freed from atop a greasy pole in the town square, then a procession of tomato-dispensing lorries push through the narrow streets. After an hour of battle, a horn sounds, everyone downs fruit — and Buñol's residents resignedly get their hoses out.

Editor's tip: It may be messy and slightly mad, but La Tomatina is so popular that it's now ticketed. Buy ahead at tomatina.es or you'll be turned away.

Charles Bridge, Prague

In a city riddled with architectural treasures — Prague's UNESCO-protected Old Town is the best-preserved medieval city in Europe — Charles Bridge is the finest of all. Completed in 1402, and for more than 400 years the only way across the River Vltava, the quarter-mile of cobbles is entered via magnificent Gothic towers at either end, with 30 ancient statues guarding its length. Come at dawn and you might have it to yourself — with hot *trdelník* pastries the essential breakfast from stalls along Karlova street.

Editor's tip: Riverside bars and Pilsner tents in the park make summer a good time to visit; but winter is even more magical, with mist clinging to the cobbled lanes, locals defrosting in cosy pubs, and the tourist hordes yet to arrive.

Shibden Valley, Calderdale, England

Countryside doesn't come more green and pleasant than that surrounding Shibden House in West Yorkshire. An hour's yomp from Halifax, among Calderdale's rollercoaster hills and valleys, it's a jumble of wild woodland, neat gardens and terraced orchards, all topped with a mock-Tudor mansion that's been here since the 1400s (it received an eccentric makeover 400 years later, thanks to owner Anne Lister, a pioneering gay woman who topped it off with battlements, beams and turrets, while writing secret, coded diaries). Wander the area in early May, following its old packhorse tracks and field-skimming paths, and you'll encounter blankets of bluebells.

Editor's tip: Stay in lively market town Hebden Bridge (20 minutes' drive): it's got galleries, antiques shops and an arthouse cinema, plus plenty of posh B&Bs. Or opt for the chocolate-box charms of Ripponden village, in the bottle-green Ryburn Valley.

Carnival, Rio de Janeiro

Feathers, spangles and flesh as far as the eye can see; giant hummingbirds; pyrotechnics; ear-ringing drummers; hip-slinking dancers... Welcome to one of the greatest spectacles on Earth: Rio Carnival. It's not the thronged street-party you might expect, though. Sure, it's a huge knees-up — the exuberant samba music continues into the small hours — but one that got so big they built a stadium for it, the Sambódromo. Now, the competing samba schools, each with its own fiercely devoted supporters, parade

in all their glory along a 700m runway between grandstands. Stand 9 is the only one with allocated seating, but 5 and 7 have views almost as good, tickets half the price (from around £50), and lashings more local atmosphere. Just wriggle your way into a good spot.

Editor's tip: You don't have to settle for spectating — you can take part, too. Sign up for about £100 via the official website, which has tons of information on the whole shebang (rio-carnival.net).

Los Angeles, USA

It's not all tours of movie lots and A-list homes in La-La Land: though clearly a beacon for the genetically-blessed, the city has something for *everyone*. The once dodgy Downtown district is now gritty-cool, from its revamped bars and restaurants, to edgy galleries. Then there are the beaches: huge swathes of pristine sand, each with its own character (compare chic Manhattan Beach with the steroid-pumped craziness of Venice, for example). Love clean-living? Hike through the hills and eat at a plethora of vegan restaurants.

Prefer calories and cocktails? Pay homage to cultish In-N-Out Burger for the best buns in town, then hang out at the dive bars in the hip Silver Lake neighbourhood. Add world-class museums and some fantastic live music venues to the mix, and you'll see that the City of Angels has plenty for the rest of us too.

Editor's tip: Factor in LA's traffic jams when deciding where to stay. Anywhere off the perpetually clogged Interstate 405 is best avoided.

Whitsunday Islands, Australia

Captain Cook was clearly running low on names to sprinkle upon the Queensland coast when he sailed through this cluster of empty, beach-fringed islands on the seventh Sunday after Easter in 1770. But the warm, shallow waters he dubbed Whitsunday Passage have since become a byword for Aussie paradise. The ocean itself is a playground for yachts and catamarans, while seaplanes skim in to land like gigantic seabirds, offloading visitors on the castaway beaches of its 74 outcrops. The star of the set is Whitsunday Island itself: thrillingly uninhabited, it's where you'll find Whitehaven Beach (pictured), draped along the island's southeast coast like a white silk scarf.

Editor's tip: Spring in the Antipodes (our autumn) brings warm, breezy weather and clear blue skies. It's a good time to see humpback whales, and you'll dodge the stinging jellyfish that plague these waters from November to April.

Oktoberfest, Munich

A chair-o-plane at a beer festival sounds like madness. But it seems the Bavarians can cope with a bellyful of lager at 11 revolutions a minute (you might prefer to give it a whirl *before* drinking any alcohol, though). You might also appreciate the chance to sit down — tables at the 16-day knees-up sell out months in advance (oktoberfest.de), and if you can't find a free bench in one of the beer tents, you won't be able buy a beer. On the plus side, you'll get drunk on the views from up there: Munich's spires rise and fall like a zoetrope, and the neon-lit Theresienwiese fairground flashes against distant white Alpine peaks.

Editor's tip: You can always try to blag a place on someone else's table: don the traditional *lederhosen* (men) or *dirndl* (ladies) — for sale on site — then hover; if you're lucky, the friendly Germans will appreciate your efforts and welcome you to join them for a *stein*.

Okavango, Botswana

They might not look menacing, but the African buffalo in this picture are far-from-gentle giants. Weighing up to 700kg and nicknamed the 'Black Death', they gained their place in the Big Five thanks to a reputation for turning on would-be hunters and charging in counter-attack. Still, approached by jeep, with cameras rather than guns, they're calm and spectacular to watch — especially in the Botswanan summer (November-March), when the grass is plentiful and herd numbers can top 1,000. Be sure to save some pixels for Okavango's other wildlife, though: elephant, lion, crocodile, rhino and wild dog are among the species found on its sprawling plains.

Editor's tip: You'll get reduced rates on the region's pricey camps by booking last-minute (less than two weeks before travel). Call direct and be prepared to bargain.

The Bungle Bungles, Australia

A secret from the outside world until 1983, the strange, orange and black mounds of this mountain range were accidentally discovered by a documentary film crew and promptly turned into one of The Kimberley's busiest attractions. Things had been rather sleepier before that — the local Aboriginal people had traversed the range on foot for 40,000 years, enjoying the abundance of animal and plant life during the rainy season. Novices might prefer to see the mountains from the air, catching a helicopter flight over caves scrawled with ancient rock art, palm-sprouting gorges, deserted lakes, and neat clusters of bee-striped mountains (a consequence of gravel and sandstone compacting together).

Editor's tip: The park is only open in dry season (April to November, subject to weather conditions).

Khao Phing Kan, Thailand

This rocky outcrop just north of Phuket often goes by a more memorable moniker — James Bond Island. Thanks to a starring role in *The Man With The Golden Gun*, it's a popular stop-off for visitors hoping to relive Roger Moore and Britt Ekland's romps across perfect beaches and through dense jungle, in hot pursuit of evil assassin Francisco Scaramanga. The location may be as dramatic as the film, but a visit by boat makes for a sublimely serene day (without a baddie in sight). Cruise across a mouthwash-green sea, below cliffs that drip limestone like huge drops of wax, and into bays of banana-yellow sand, shaded by palm umbrellas.

Editor's tip: You can't overnight here, but stay on the neighbouring island of Yao Noi for empty beaches with unforgettable, island-strewn views of Phang Nga Bay.

The Nile, Egypt

Stretching almost 7,000km across Africa, from Egypt to Burundi, the Nile is so vast that explorers are *still* searching for its most distant sources. The Egyptian stretch takes up a fifth of its length, and life on the water has changed little across the centuries: *feluccas*, the wooden sailing boats pictured here, have been ploughing the waters since ancient times, propelled by nothing more than the breeze and the current. Sail in one from Aswan to Luxor, past age-old towns and temples, and it's like a slow meander into an exotic past.

Editor's tip: A *felucca* trip is the definition of slow travel. Most take two or three days, but you'll need to factor in at least one day's wriggle-room for your journey, as you're at the mercy of the tides and the wind.

Las Teresitas, Tenerife

Shhh, don't reveal the Canaries' biggest secret: plenty of Tenerife is gloriously unspoilt. Take this beach on the island's northern finger, a short drive from the capital, Santa Cruz: a boomerang of imported Saharan sand, Las Teresitas is bookended by the fishing village of San Andrés on one side and a simple stone jetty at the other, where the sand runs out and the ocean begins. Drive away from the coast, and you're soon on the winding roads of the Anaga mountains, where forested peaks face off with tiny villages and myriad hiking trails cat's-cradle through the landscape. This is a Tenerife you won't find in the travel agent's brochures — serene, empty and ripe for exploration.

Editor's tip: San Andrés has some of the best seafood restaurants on the island. Try La Posada del Pez, but book ahead as it's popular with locals (especially on Sundays). And wherever you eat, try local speciality, *papas arrugadas*. The translation — 'wrinkly potatoes' — may not sound appealing, but the salty side dish is addictive.

Holi Festival, India

Did someone turn up the contrast settings? India pulsates with colour any day of the year, but when Holi comes around, the country erupts in a burst of polychrome brilliance, heralding spring and the Hindu New Year. Holi commemorates the blue-skinned god Krishna's efforts to win the love of the goddess Radha: fearing she would reject him for his colouring, Krishna painted Radha's face, too. Today people flood the streets to fling fluorescent paint or dust at one another, symbolising a fresh start. Leave your best clothes at home (whatever you wear will end up stained), pick up your supply of powders in one of the markets — then follow the crowds.

Editor's tip: Holi usually falls around mid-March, but states celebrate for different lengths of time — check your location and its dates before booking flights or accommodation. And be aware that celebrations are more raucous in the north, and best in Uttar Pradesh (northeast), where Krishna is believed to have grown up. You'll find the most full-on revelry happens in Agra (luckily for travellers, that's also home to the Taj Mahal).

Wormsloe Plantation, Georgia, USA

This shady, oak-lined avenue looks the epitome of peace. But at its very end, three kilometres from the dirt-smudged entrance gate, lies the ruined mansion of Noble Jones, a man whose turbulent life was typical of his time. Arriving in Georgia with the first English settlers in 1733, the carpenter battled starvation to reinvent himself as a doctor, policeman, and go-between to the Native Americans and British royalty. Today, crumbling, grey ruins are all that remain of his once great house, but meandering trails head out through fairytale forest towards photo-opp views over Savannah's historic district, 15 minutes' drive away — and the country lanes that lead to a hundred other beautiful colonial curiosities.

Editor's tip: Base yourself in one of the converted mansions (now hotels) in Savannah's centre. You'll get grand rooms *and* Southern hospitality.

Kuala Lumpur, Malaysia

Ten thousand lanterns illuminate Thean Hou temple during its Chinese New Year celebrations, making it a dazzling place to join the festivities. The lights have meaning as well as aesthetic appeal: the red part represents happiness, and the gold part wealth. Find out if you're destined for either, by having your fortune told at one of the temple's stalls. Or simply revel in the good fortune of being *here*: Thean Hou at festival time is a once-in-a-lifetime assault on the senses, complete with acrobats, warrior monks and dragon dancers alongside rooftop sculptures of roaring dragons and psychedelic birds.

Editor's tip: Travelling in Asia around Chinese New Year (typically mid-February) can be hectic. Expect long airport queues and packed trains and buses. Book whatever you can (even meals) before leaving the UK.

Amalfi Coast, Italy

You want subtle? Forget the Amalfi Coast. Craggy green-carpeted hills, dropping off into aquamarine blue; crayon-box-hued villages clustered onto precipitous slopes; sea-hugging hairpin roads made for driving with the top down — it's *operatically* beautiful. So no wonder it's such a draw for celebs (and tourists seeking a glimpse of them): the picturesque streets of jumbled old towns such as Positano get clogged in summer. But you can escape the crowds by ascending the hills in springtime to jewel-box Ravello, home to a pretty church, fragrant blooms, and cypress trees. You'll get this view, perfectly framed by an umbrella pine tree, from the garden of Villa Rufolo.

Editor's tip: The coast road gets crazy-busy in summer, so consider taking one of the regular local buses. Travel west to east and snag a window seat for Tyrrhenian Sea views.

Quiraing, Isle of Skye

If Sergio Leone (Mr Spaghetti Western) had ever decided to direct a Viking film, this craggy patch of northern Skye — whipped up by a prehistoric landslip — would have made a worthy setting. Lying just off Scotland's wild west coast, its towering cliffs, rugged rocky pinnacles, and dramatic lighting effects make for a cinematic backdrop. In the days of Viking raids, the island's cattle farmers (shall we call them cowboys?) would drive their animals up to a flat expanse of grass called 'the table', hiding them behind a ridge of jutting cliffs to keep them away from the rustling Norsemen. That 'table' is one of the highlights of the 7km hiking trail you can follow into the Quiraing peaks, where you'll get all-conquering views of this frontier landscape.

Editor's tip: The Quiraing walk is 'Hard' difficulty (isleofskye.com), and changeable weather can catch you off-guard; pack a waterproof and fleece.

Festival of the Sahara, Tunisia

Just beyond the palm-fringed gates of Douz — a sleepy, sandstone town in central Tunisia — the Sahara sprawls into seeming endlessness, edged by empty, neon skies. It's an unforgettable sight at any time of year, but in mid-winter, when the International Festival of the Sahara comes to town, it's a once-in-a-lifetime spectacle. Over four days, more than 100,000 people from across Africa congregate to celebrate Bedouin culture, exploding onto the silent landscape with camel races, hypnotic Berber dances and daring horseback acrobatics.

Editor's tip: If you want to do it properly, ignore Douz's mediocre hotels in favour of one of the Bedouin-style camps around an hour's drive into the desert. Try Campement Zmela, where you can try star-gazing by night or dune-buggying by day, and return to incredible local home-cooked dishes.

Dubai, UAE

There are no half measures in Dubai. You want skiing? Ski Dubai is the biggest indoor ski resort in the world. Shops? The Dubai Mall has 1,200 to choose from. As for skyscrapers, the 163-floor Burj Khalifa (the tallest building in the world; pictured) is 828m high – that's more than two and a half times the height of London's Shard. A desert backwater until oil was discovered in 1966, Dubai is now the UAE's capital of excess — enjoying 20°C+ temperatures when back home we're scraping ice off the pavement.

Editor's tip: For a glimpse of pre-mall Dubai, visit the souks, a joyous jumble of spice and jewel stalls either side of The Creek. And make time to experience the desert: it's just 45 minutes from downtown, but camping in the dunes is a memory that will stay with you forever.

Samburu National Park, Rift Valley, Kenya

Known by their neighbours as the 'butterfly folk' thanks to their brightly coloured clothes, the semi-nomadic Samburu people wander northern Kenya's stretch of the Great Rift Valley, moving their livestock towards fresh pasture every few weeks, and maintaining centuries-old traditions in the face of modernity. In this remote region, where dusty desert and grassland abut dense forest, the plains come striped with zebra, while giraffes peep through the trees and pink flamingos dot the lakes. Visitors can stay in one of several lodges run in conjunction with the Samburu, who act as guides on drives to spot lions, black rhinos, elephants, hyenas and leopards.

Editor's tip: For true immersion, consider a week-long camel safari, walking (or riding) between temporary camps with a Samburu guide, and visiting villages along the way.

Neuschwanstein Castle, Bavaria, Germany

It may look like a land far, far away, where a kiss could wake a snoozing princess, but the snow-tipped turrets of Neuschwanstein aren't make-believe: in fact, the castle is less than two hours from Munich. The Romanesque-style inspiration for the fortress in Walt Disney's *Sleeping Beauty* was commissioned in the 1800s by the young, 'mad' King Ludwig II. Now it's open to the public, though you will need to put in some leg work: it's a 15-minute climb from the nearest bus stop, and there are 200 more stairs inside. It's all worth it, though, for the balcony views of the fairytale Alpsee lake and the Alps beyond.

Editor's tip: Landscapes don't get more sparklingly seasonal than this, and snow isn't the only reason to visit in winter. In January and February, *Fasching* — Germany's jolly carnival season — is in full swing.

Seventy Islands, Palau

There's been no sneaky Photoshopping here — the water really is this blue, and the trees really are this green. (And that's exactly why it makes the pages of this book.) Seventy Islands is an archipelago of forest-smothered limestone and pristine coral in the Pacific; marine life loves the place, which means scuba divers do, too. Those of a nervous (or, indeed, normal) disposition, however, may wish to avoid Shark City, where shark-hunting is banned — which means coming nose-to-nose with a hammerhead is a distinct possibility. Want to play it safe? Catch this dreamy view on a helicopter tour instead (rockislandhelicopters.com; book well ahead).

Editor's tip: Take a boat to the Big Drop Off to dive or snorkel in one of 60 amazing vertical dive shafts (palau-impac.com, which can also organise the special permit necessary). Expect much nibbling of toes — the fish here aren't afraid to say hello.

The Treasury, Petra, Jordan

Lit by dozens of candles that turn the pink rock fiery orange, Petra's Treasury appears like a gateway to the underworld. And, in a way, it is. Built as a crypt in the 1st century AD, it takes its name — Al-Khazneh, meaning 'Treasury' — from the apocryphal story that Bedouin bandits used it as a safe store for their loot. (Steven Spielberg was obviously convinced; he used it as the final resting place of the Holy Grail in his *Indiana Jones and the Last Crusade*.) In fact, it's just one of several staggering sites spread across this 2,300-year-old rock-hewn Nabatean city (look out for the monastery and amphitheatre, too). The Treasury itself is never more numinous than when lit up with candles, like a giant altarpiece, every Monday, Wednesday and Thursday night.

Editor's tip: The hike to the monastery isn't easy (it includes 1,000-plus sandstone steps), especially if you're travelling during the summer, but it's worth it for the sensational vista, just beyond. It's not called 'The End Of The World View' for nothing...

Moscow, Russia

Not *all* Russian icons are religious. In fact, our favourites are available to buy on half the street corners in Moscow — and are wearable. As early as October, a rabbit-fur *ushanka* hat is a sensible purchase, ensuring head-and-ear protection from the plummeting temperatures. Popularised by the military during the Great Patriotic War of 1941 (since helmets offered insufficient insulation), they are ubiquitous standard wear today — and sold in stores citywide for anything up to £75. Equally iconic, *Matryoshka* ('little matron') nesting dolls are essential buys, too: inspired by forerunners from the Far East, these are made from birch with a distinctive lacquered sheen and cartoonish guises, from female-folkloric to celebrity-satirical. Old Arbat Street is the magnet for tourist shoppers, but Izmailovsky Market has perhaps more appeal, with piles of fleamarket finds to rummage through.

Editor's tip: The Moscow Metro is cheap, easy to use and its beautiful ornate stations are a sight in themselves; explore the 'brown' circle line in particular.

Tikal, Guatemala

Choked by 575 dense, rainforesty square kilometres of jungle, the almost futuristic temple complex of Tikal was in fact built between the 2nd and 9th centuries by the Mayans as a city for around 60,000 people. Only a fraction of the jaguar- and puma-dotted landscape has been excavated so far; finds include the steely Great Jaguar Temple, a king's burial place (yet 47m tall), and Temple V (57m!). But for this view? Clamber up the steep wooden stairs at towering Temple IV (65m), and breathe in the forest-fresh air, keeping eyes peeled for toucans and monkeys in the canopy.

Editor's tip: Stay overnight in Flores, around an hour's drive away, and take the first bus to get to Tikal for sunrise (opens 6am). Tikal National Park is busiest from around 10am to 2pm, but you'll need a full day to do the site justice.

Richmond Park, England

Just after dawn on misty autumn mornings, there's a stirring in London's rambling Richmond Park. More than a stirring, in fact: a riotous clash, as hundreds of red stags and fallow bucks battle — knocking antlers, barking and roaring — among the fiery foliage to gain the attention of potential mates. Known as The Rut, this violent, sometimes lethal, display of love-sick males has taken place since at least 1637, when the park was established as a royal hunting ground. Do stroll through the 1,000 hectares, a catalogue of crisp yellows and burnished oranges this time of year, but keep your distance — at least 50m — from the deer. When the sun burns the clouds away, make for the park's highest point, King Henry's Mound, to spy majestic St Paul's Cathedral, 16km away.

Editor's tip: Come in sun-kissed May, June or July for the chance to spot nursing mothers with their young. Bring binoculars, and give them an extra-wide berth.

Angkor Wat, Cambodia

If the remains of this 12th-century kingdom look filmic, it's probably because they've had starring roles in everything from *Tomb Raider* to *Indiana Jones*. But though popular parts of the complex can get bottlenecked with visitors (especially Ta Prohm, where Angelina Jolie did her business), the site is 200 hectares and you'll always find an empty slice of ruin on which to sit and ruminate. It's not just ancient history here: among the intricate carvings of seven-headed serpents and dancing goddesses, there is graffiti from the time of the Khmer Rouge — a reminder of how far Cambodia's come in just 25 years.

Editor's tip: Avoid temple fatigue by breaking up days in the complex with time in Siem Reap. This satellite town is delightfully moreish, serving up cool coffee houses and a string of riverside rice-wine bars.

Hawkdun Range, New Zealand

It's hard to believe, as you watch the sky turn pink over the peaceful Hawkdun Range, that these mountains were ever the site of feverish activity. But there was 'gold in them thar hills', and in the 1860s this sleepy corner of New Zealand's South Island was overrun with prospectors. The Gold Rush years may now be a distant memory, but if you visit in winter (UK summer), exploring the mountain trails on skis or skating on the frozen lakes and ponds, you'll almost certainly feel you've struck gold. In July, if the ice is thick enough, you can even watch Bonspiel curling at the frozen Idaburn Dam — or have a go yourself at the Indoor Curling Rink in Naseby.

Editor's tip: Despite those 'back-of-beyond' looks, you won't have to go far off-route to see the Hawkduns: Route 8 to ever-popular Queenstown skirts them.

Keyhole Arch, California

Poseidon's personal tanning booth? No, this is an all-natural phenomenon — visible on the rare occasions when the setting sun aligns with the wave-carved window in this rock. And it's no place for winter sunbathing: this is Big Sur, a rugged swathe of the California coast refrigerated by mists that roll in off the Pacific. So you'll want to wrap up warm for the climax at around 6pm: as the blood-orange sun makes contact with the horizon, the blaze of light flares momentarily as it bounces off the water's surface, before being slowly and stunningly extinguished.

Editor's tip: This light show can only be witnessed for a brief period from the beginning of January. Unsurprisingly, it's a magnet for photographers, so make sure you arrive with plenty of time to stake out your space and set up your tripod.

Teahupoo, Tahiti

Waves can rise to seven metres off the shore of this tiny village in southern Tahiti. Add tiger sharks and sharp coral reef and you have a break that's strictly for surf pros (Billabong holds an annual competition here, as part of the World Championship Tour). But though braving the water can bring on an adrenaline rush of epic proportions, the hypnotic waves actually have the *opposite* effect when seen from the shore. Stay in one of the serene bungalow resorts hidden in the hills above the beach, and you'll be soothed by a view of lush rainforest tumbling towards the sea's sparkle, as well as the somnolent sound of the surf.

Editor's tip: An hour's drive northwest of Teahupoo, the dramatic black sand beach at Papara is the nearest Tahiti comes to beginners' surfing territory. You can book lessons here, but check the conditions first, as waves can get too big.

Amsterdam

Sometimes known as the 'Dancing Houses', for the way they appear to lean merrily against one another, like slow dancers at the end of a party, these buildings overlooking Amsterdam's central Damrak canal have some stories to tell — around 400 years' worth, in fact. First built for the fat-cat diamond merchants, shipbuilders and spice traders who made the city the financial capital of the world in the 17th century, they've since survived wars and floods, seen winters that turned canals into ice-rinks, and summers bloom technicolour with tulips. Today the houses play a starring role as the subject of most people's first photos of the city, as they spill out from nearby Centraal Station along Damrak's cobbled waterfront.

Editor's tip: On the *other* side of Centraal Station from the Damrak, ferries take pedestrians across the IJ to hip, industrial Amsterdam-Noord for free.

Sossusvlei, Namib Desert, Namibia

Boer settlers said a man cries twice in the Namib — once when he arrives, once when he leaves. It's the sheer scale of the place that blows you away: haul yourself up the Sossusvlei dunes, gawp at the ocean of sand cresting silently toward the sea, and you'll know exactly what the old Boers meant. The world's oldest desert takes an elemental grip on your soul, but Namibia isn't all desert and dunes: its Atlantic coastline is a windswept wilderness of seal colonies, shipwrecks and wetland reserves, with the salt pans of Etosha and the ancient wilds of Damaraland offering stunning inland safari, too.

Editor's tip: Your best Sossusvlei base is Wolwedans Dune Camp, a staggeringly remote retreat with six Tarzan-chic tents built right into the side of a 250m dune.

Giant's Causeway, Northern Ireland

Legend has it that this rocky, rubbly honeycomb path was created when the Northern Irish giant Finn McCool decided to battle a Scottish enemy, and threw rocks into the sea to create a passage between them. (In the end, the other fellow was so big that our hero ran home and hid, disguised as a baby.) A more scientific theory suggests that the causeway is the result of cracking tectonic plates causing molten magma to rise to the Earth's surface, 60 million years ago. Still, there's a mysterious feel to these hexagonal bits of basalt at the very tip of Northern Ireland, plus huge holidaying potential in the beautiful Antrim countryside that surrounds them.

Editor's tip: The 190km Causeway Coastal Route is a spectacular stretch, wriggling from Londonderry to Belfast via empty beaches, cutesy harbours and ruined castles. Don't miss The Gobbins — an exhilarating, cliff-hugging coastal path.

Damnoen Saduak Floating Market, Bangkok

It's early morning on the Damnoen Saduak canal in the Thai capital, and the air is infused with scents drifting from the sunlit water. Elderly women wield wooden spatulas, pushing sizzling dumplings across wide-bottomed pans. Men sell papayas and scarlet lychees for handfuls of baht, passing their wares carefully from boat to boat. Floating markets such as this are a staple of Thai life, a legacy of the communities that used to live by the water, growing their crops and piling them into boats each morning to sell to villages up and down the river. Travellers now haggle for souvenirs alongside Thais bargaining for beans and mangoes, but all converge on the street-food boats, lured by plates of pleasingly sticky satay or bowls of slurpable noodle soup.

Editor's tip: To avoid the tourist hordes at their worst, visit early on a weekday morning. You'll breakfast in peace with the regulars, on coconut pancakes and iced sweet tea. Buses 78 and 996 depart Bangkok's Southern Bus terminal to Damnoen Saduak (it's a two-hour trip).

Lion Rock, Hong Kong

Even by mega-city standards, Hong Kong is *hectic*. So it's just as well it's blessed with enough green space for everyone to take a breather. Yes, you should squeeze onto the tram up to Victoria Peak to admire the views from Hong Kong island — but you won't be the only one up there by a long way. So to get right away from it all, lace up your walking shoes and take a hike up to Lion Rock Country Park, on the Kowloon side of Victoria Harbour. And come at evening time for the most dramatic view, when this electrifying urban jungle turns slowly into a twinkly light show.

Editor's tip: Cab rides in Hong Kong are cheap, so save your legs en route to Lion Rock by getting a taxi from Wong Tai Sin or Diamond Hill MTR station to the Lion Pavilion on Sha Tin Pass Road. Follow the MacLehose Trail from there.

The Maldives

You might think you know what you're getting with these frequently photographed supermodels of travel. But the Indian Ocean islands' perfection on first bird's-eye glance — the halo of pale aquamarine around vanilla beaches, arcing wooden walkways unspooling out to over-water villas — still elicits gasps. If the plane view feels like a lottery win, you know you've taken the *big* prize once you step onto the torch-lit jetty, then chalky-soft sand lapped by crystal shallows. From here, your to-do list shrinks to the length of a haiku. First, a walk around the island perimeter (usually accomplished in half an hour); then it's beach vs pool, spa vs snorkelling, sunset yoga vs cocktails... until at night, after sultry dinners beside moonlight-diffusing sea, you're rocked to sleep by the sound of wavelets and that rehab-like routine.

Editor's tip: Only BA flies direct from the UK to the Maldives (and only in winter; 10 hours). Connecting flights (Emirates, Qatar, Etihad, Sri Lankan) are cheaper but take 3-4 hours more.

Dubrovnik, Croatia

Once beloved of poets and painters (Byron called it the 'Pearl of the Adriatic'), today Dubrovnik is a muse to the world's film crews. Stage-set good-looking, its marble streets invite you to wander past doorways you imagine might open to reveal the whole thing as just a facade. It's not only looks that have landed the place roles in shows such as *Game of Thrones*, though. The city's got a good-time side, too: among its domes and bell towers, its outbursts of Gothic, Renaissance and Baroque, Dubrovnik also has one of the world's most beautiful bars, Buza (Crijevićeva Street),

with chairs perched on rocks above the Adriatic. *Too* pretty? Take a walk around the city's medieval walls of golden stone for a view of washing lines and kitchen windows that's every bit as appealing as the big-screen scenes.

Editor's tip: Enjoy Dubrovnik in peace on an evening stroll after the cruise-ship crowds have left — the city walls are open until 7pm in high summer. The light is great then, too, picking out the oranges and pinks of this storybook skyline.

Wat Muang, Thailand

Years of meditation might allow this monk to stroll serenely towards the enormous statue of Buddha, but the rest of us may not be able to play it so cool: whichever direction you approach from, the 92m figure — Thailand's largest, almost as tall as the Statue of Liberty — rears up excitingly from the surrounding plains. Wat Muang, the Buddha's temple home, has a few more surprises up its sleeve, too: a giant lotus so big it contains a golden temple building; mirrored chambers that appear to stretch to infinity; and a grisly garden of statues depicting Buddhist hell. And then you're faced with the Big Buddha himself: join worshippers climbing the stairs to reach up to his middle finger, dangling tantalisingly close to the ground.

Editor's tip: Wat Muang is only 80km north of Bangkok but isn't easy to reach; take a train or bus to Ang Thong or UNESCO-protected Ayutthaya, then a private or shared taxi.

Alkmaar tulip fields, Netherlands

Seen from above it looks like a colourful carpet. But peer more closely and you'll see this 'rug' is woven entirely of flowers. From mid-March to mid-May, the plains around Alkmaar, north of Amsterdam, are transformed into a technicolour blanket, as first crocuses, then daffodils, and finally tulips, come into bloom. It's not just a pretty picture, though — there's some serious money to be made in horticulture, and tulips were once so profitable, their bulbs were used as currency in the 17th century. Four hundred years on, the tourists who flock to Alkmaar to cycle and snap their way around its psychedelic countryside might do their transactions in euros, but one thing's clear: flowers are still very much part of the tapestry of life in these parts.

Editor's tip: The best way to get to Alkmaar is via Amsterdam, 40 minutes away by train.

Pamukkale, Turkey

Turkey's Turquoise Coast is synonymous with beach resorts and cobalt coves, but it's three hours *inland* that you'll find Pamukkale — the region's spectacular star. Meaning 'Cotton Castle' in Turkish, Pamukkale is a blindingly white travertine terrace, an ethereal cascade of limestone thermal pools, formed by millennia of hot spring deposits from the Anatolian plateau. Walk up the marbled path through the Byzantine gates (shoes off, so bring a bag), then make like a Roman at Hierapolis, a superbly preserved Greek-Roman ruined city right by the falls, where you can bathe (bring swimming costume, too) in a 36°C pool with fragments of ancient marble columns submerged in its raki-clear, mineral depths.

Editor's tip: Stay overnight and visit first thing to avoid the cruise ship and coach parties who arrive from Kuşadasi in the early afternoon.

Namolokama, Kaua'i, Hawaii

No, this isn't the setting for a Herbal Essences advert (yet). It's just another tropical cascade in the lush northern region of Kaua'i island. Before the rains, the 1,300m Namolokama Mountain rustles drily with bamboo and ferns. But after the heavens have opened, dozens of waterfalls spring to life, thundering down the ancient lava-rock slopes. For the best (and driest) perspective, book into a suite at The Westin Princeville Ocean Resort Villas where, from your private patio, you can watch the formation of up to 20 cascades. After the clouds have dispersed, go for a closer look while the torrents still flow (find hikes at trails.com), yomping up a hillside perfumed with the scent of ginger and plumeria flowers.

Editor's tip: This part of Kaua'i is one of the rainiest places on the planet — don't forget to take a brolly.

Cape Town, South Africa

As summer in South Africa draws to an end, and warm air from the Indian Ocean meets cooler currents off the South Atlantic, Cape Town puts on quite a climatic show: low-flying cloud drapes itself like dry ice around the flanks of Lion's Head Mountain, while below, vague amid the opalescent vapour, the city appears like footlights, playing up Nature's extravaganza. These special effects don't just look good, they do good: February heralds the fruition of the grape-growing season, and while it may be witheringly hot and dry on the coast, those cooling air currents work magic on vineyards spread over the surrounding hills, helping maintain the perfect temperature for long and leisurely ripening. Raise your glass.

Editor's tip: The clouds are beautiful, but can be dangerous. If you plan on taking a hike up Lion's Head or Table Mountain, avoid windy days, when fog can appear out of nowhere.

Songkran Water Festival, Thailand

Something takes hold of the usually reserved Thai people at their biggest national festival, Songkran. The Thai New Year marks the end of the sweltering hot season and the beginning of the monsoon, as rain cools the air, and rice paddies flood and flourish. In the past, Songkran was celebrated with the flick of a few drops into the face of a friend, but over the years it has gradually evolved into the all-out water fight it is today. As streets from Bangkok to the bustling north bake in 35°C heat, kids and grown-ups alike drench each other by the bucket-load — or wait in ambush with bazooka-sized water pistols.

Editor's tip: Songkran happens once a year: April. And while it's hot and sticky in the cities, it's a great time to visit Thailand's coasts and islands, with only a few off-season tourists on those creamy palm-shaded beaches.

Cape Verde

There's no discernible reason why the mega-brand, mega-buck hotels have stayed away from Cape Verde, the string of 10 desert-island dollops 500km off the coast of Senegal. But there might be limited time to get there before they arrive. Consider the islands' attractions: wild Santo Antão, where rainforest undulates across mountains and valleys, trimmed in neatly terraced farmland and remote villages; fiery Fogo, with its lunar-esque, volcanic landscape topped with an incongruously cute, pastel-painted capital, São Filipe; Boa Vista, with kilometre upon kilometre of deserted sand on beaches just like this one; and sprawling Santiago, home to the UNESCO Heritage Site of Cidade Velha – the oldest colonial town in the Tropics.

Editor's tip: Avoid Sal, owing to its badly done package resorts. Try Santo Antão and Boa Vista, for their handful of simple and chic guesthouses.

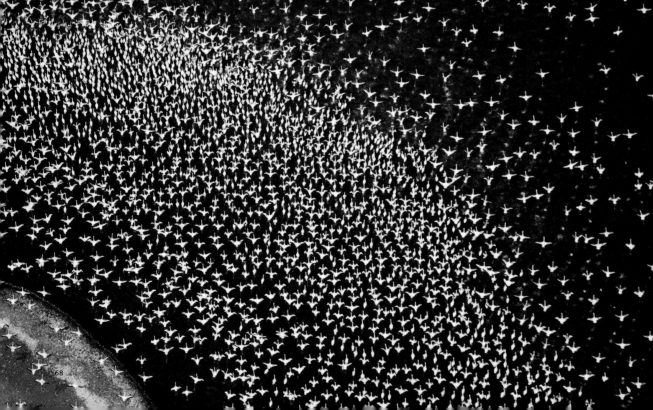

Arc de Triomphe, Paris

Your sweaty brow and aching calves may not epitomise Parisian chic, but by the time you climb the 284 steps to the top of Paris's iconic Arc de Triomphe, you won't be worried about people looking at you. The surrounding avenues radiate towards the grand Neo-Classical arch, accentuating the majestic allure of its captivating 1836 contours. The views from the top — across glistening golden domes, wispy chimney smoke, and the steely statuesque Eiffel Tower — are magical any time of day, but L'Arc stays open later than most of the city's other sights (closing time varies between 10.30pm and 11pm). So head there an hour before it shuts, when the queues are quieter, and you might have the view to yourself.

Editor's tip: Do Paris in spring for crisp, sunny days, long nights, and the lure of an aperitif in a cosy bar — it's a recipe for romance. It's also one of the cheapest times of the year to visit, as long as you avoid Valentine's Day and Easter.

Lake Bogoria, Kenya

Sometimes the glamorous stars of wildlife documentaries can be elusive. But not here. At Lake Bogoria, in the Rift Valley, a million pink flamingos pack in as tightly as commuters on a train. They're here for lunch, dining on the algae that flourish at the shores of this thermally charged lake, somehow dodging its scalding geysers that erupt up to five metres high. And with standing-room-only in the shallows, the leggy birds don't have room for a running take-off, so any disturbance — a passing truck, or a hyena, say — creates a sort of avian Mexican wave, as undulations of pink feathers ripple spectacularly away from the shore. When to go? Late July to early August is the peak time: that's when Lake Bogoria's algae is at its richest after the rainy season.

Editor's tip: Nearby Lake Baringo has the best places to stay. We rate Island Camp (islandcamp.com) — the hotel will pack a picnic for flamingo-watching guests going to Lake Bogoria. You can also take nature walks with the in-house guide, to spot fish eagles, giraffes and hippos.

Svalbard, Norway

He *could* just be admiring the view... But it's more likely that this polar bear is scanning the water for his dinner: seal, served on a bed of ice. That's by far the favourite dish in Svalbard, a freezing archipelago marking the halfway point between the North Pole and mainland Norway — and a place where the bear population has actually risen by more than 40 per cent since 2004. The best way to see these white giants is by boat, cruising the fjords in the white-out of the region's night-less summer — and spotting walrus, whales and thousands of seabirds, too.

Editor's tip: Between May and September, the ice melts enough to make the Arctic Ocean navigable to some pretty cushy cruise ships — but if you're more about bears than buffets, opt for a smaller boat that can get you to Svalbard's harder-to-reach corners.

Zaanse Schans, Netherlands

At first glance it's as if you've stepped straight into a work by Jacob van Ruisdael, the landscape painter of the Dutch Golden Age: sky a honeyed blue, dabbed with creamy clouds; sunlight gilding the sails of windmills; flat horizon reflected in the high waters of a canal... But in reality, Zaanse Schans is nothing like a painting. Not that it's not pretty — it's every bit as bucolic as it appears here — but it's also a year-round hive of activity. The windmills spin in the breeze to grind cocoa, spices and paint powders; there are liquor distilleries, cheese-makers and clog-carvers all hard at work; cyclists jangle along the dykes. And all the while, the canal teems with traffic, providing an aquatic highway for private barges and tourist boats alike.

Editor's tip: Go in spring, which sees an explosion of colour, from the Keukenhof tulip fields, to the Koningsdag festival, when revellers clad in orange hit the streets celebrating the birth of King Willem-Alexander.

The Glacier Express, Swiss Alps

It's billed as the world's slowest express train. But 'most beautiful' would be equally applicable, because for its entire seven-and-a-half-hour run, the Glacier Express winds through the heart of the Swiss Alps, between St Moritz and Zermatt. The crane-your-neck scenery is continuous and all-enveloping — and, conveniently enough, the carriage windows arch right up to the roof to give you a 360° view. Crawling like a flame-red caterpillar, the train rumbles through 91 tunnels and over 291 bridges, among them the Landwasser Viaduct, pictured here, which takes the line teetering across a narrow gorge, before burrowing through a sheer cliff.

Editor's tip: Finish in Zermatt rather than St Moritz. Crouched beneath the twisted spike of the Matterhorn, the former is by far the more dramatic climax to the trip. And bear in mind it's easy to integrate the Glacier Express into a longer rail holiday (or ski trip), using a Swiss Rail pass.

Las Fallas Festival, Valencia, Spain

They're asking for it, every single one of them. They deserve to burn — because the tradition that started as a springtime bonfire of winter's leftover wood soon became something bigger, darker, more... explosive. See, Valencia's annual Las Fallas Festival is still about a purge of the old in celebration of the new, but in modern times that 'dead wood' takes the form of elaborate papier-mâché sculptures called *fallas*: huge, cartoon-like effigies of celebrities, politicians, members of the royal family and anyone else thought guilty — by the people — of dubious behaviour in the past year. Crowds gather in the Plaza del Ayuntamiento to experience the *mascletà*, a riot of firecrackers orchestrated to create a rhythmic composition, like a deafening drum solo. And the festival culminates at midnight, when all the *fallas* are set alight and Valencia turns orange in the flames.

Editor's tip: Get yourself a Valencia Card (valenciatouristcard.com) so you can jump on the bus or Metro to get to the *Fallas* events outside the city centre as well.

Derwent Fells,
Lake District

Pleasant pastures, mountains green, clouded hills, and those holy shafts of sunlight illuminating the gentle slopes… You'd swear William Blake had been sitting here, on Derwent Fells, when he wrote his most celebrated poem, *Jerusalem*. (Actually he was just outside Bognor Regis, which might explain the 'dark' 'Satanic' stuff.) This quiet corner of the ambrosial Buttermere valley is one of the Lake District's more serene spots, emptier than its more eminent neighbours, such as Windermere or Keswick — and, arguably, ever-so-slightly more photogenic, too.

Editor's tip: Don't fancy taking to the trails alone? The Lake District National Park Authority runs good, free guided walks throughout the year (lakedistrict.gov.uk).

Borneo, Asia

Soft hazel eyes sweeping up to meet yours, long fingers curled gracefully around a vine — a face-to-face moment with Borneo's 'old man of the Forest' is heart-swelling. There are two ways to have one: visiting a rehabilitation centre, or touring Borneo and Sumatra's rainforests. Seeing them in the wild feels more organic, but sightings can be distant and fleeting (Sabah's Danum Valley has the best odds). For a close-up, then, head to a rehab centre for feeding time. At conservation centres such as Sepilok's, rangers scatter fruit onto a forest platform within metres of you. You may be entertained by parental scoldings, juvenile tantrums, even leaves appropriated as umbrellas — but the jungle's 'stars' are still wild and wonderfully unpredictable.

Editor's tip: Fallen in love? You can volunteer at Sepilok for up to two months via travellersworldwide.com.

Sandy Spit, British Virgin Islands

Don't be surprised if the soporific theme tune to *Desert Island Discs* runs through your head as you approach this tiny uninhabited islet. A minuscule speck of green and white surrounded by turquoise waters, Sandy Spit has just two coconut palm trees to catch the warm Caribbean breeze. So what's the big draw? Oh, just the immaculate white beach and vivid coral reefs... Then, of course, there's one of the Caribbean's biggest sailing events, the BVI Spring Regatta and Sailing Festival (bvispringregatta.org), which takes place each spring. Watch the sails skimming the waves — and join in the festival's beach parties and barbecues.

Editor's tip: If you want something more than a swim and a snorkel, head just north of Sandy Spit to the Playground at Green Cay (Jost Van Dyke Island), for some of the BVIs' best diving.

Rio de Janeiro, Brazil

According to locals, after God spent six days
creating the world, He spent the seventh relaxing
in Rio — cracking open coconuts on the beach,
surfing the waves and taking in the marvellous
views. One of the best is at dawn from Tijuca
National Park, Christ silhouetted on high, the sun
orange above the rippling mountains of Niterói;
here, steamy rainforests swathe the hills above
Ipanema and Copacabana. Tours of Tijuca are
easy to book through Rio hotels or UK operators,
but don't dawdle: early birds will get a queue-
free ride on the railway that runs up to Christ the
Redeemer (tremdocorcovado.rio), toucans flitting
through the trees, marmoset monkeys small
enough to sit inside a tea cup — and crowd-free
views from its jungly lookouts.

Editor's tip: Don't miss Rio's 'new' old
centre, which glistens with innovative
museums and galleries — including the Museum
of Tomorrow (museudoamanha.org.br), a
spaceship-like pod hovering over Guanabara Bay.

Santorini, Greece

Peeking over each other like tourists jostling for the view, the buildings on Santorini's jagged clifftops edge forward to the drop; some hotels, churches and cafes are so precipitously placed that your coffee (or prayer) comes with a side of vertigo. This is the island's west, or its 'caldera', side; this is high-glamour, honeymooners' Santorini, where smoothly sculpted, white-stucco cave hotels come with grotto pools and clifftop spas, and your daintily-served fish dinner costs more than you forked out for your flights. Yet there's still a rawness to it — between snowy clusters of chic hospitality, whole stretches of cliff exist with only crumbling pathways (and hardly any handrails), and *some* sleepy tavernas still serve up the homemade classics. There's a lot beyond your infinity pool...

Editor's tip: To see an earthier side of Santorini, take a taxi from the caldera coast to Pyrgos (half an hour's drive), a spiralling walk up cobbled paths, past faded-blue doorways, and likely a donkey.

Church of the Saviour on Blood, St Petersburg

The history of this most eyeball-scorching masterpiece of Russian cathedrals has all the gruesome intrigue of a Tarantino screenplay. Legs ripped off, stomach spilling open, and face hopelessly mutilated – it was on this site in 1881 that Tsar Alexander II fell victim to assassination by bomb (it's his blood that lends the church its name). Stalin later formulated plans to blow the monument to glittery smithereens as part of his offensive against religion, but these were put on hold when World War II broke out. (The church was used as a morgue during that conflict, which claimed the lives of more than a million of the city's inhabitants.) Nowadays all the high drama comes in the form of its gleaming Italianate ceilings, each meticulously restored over three decades before the cathedral reopened to the public in 1997. A blessed relief indeed.

Editor's tip: Getting a Russian visa can be a complicated process; book through a specialist tour operator who'll take care of it for you.

Kerala, India

The beaches, plantations and rivers of India's southwestern stretch make for a thoroughly relaxing holiday — but this isn't the place to laze on a lounger. Among the myriad things to do? Navigate the backwaters by boat, to watch fishermen throwing nets from dug-out canoes, villagers washing up along the banks, and coconut palms casting dancing shadows on the labyrinthine canals, streams and lagoons. Or travel to the Western Ghats, where tea and coffee plantations squiggle through the landscape, and hill stations come adorned with white-iced churches and fragrant spice markets. Factor in time for a cookery lesson (so you can recreate the region's fragrant, subtle dishes) and an Ayurvedic treatment (the ancient healing art was born here), and you'll only just have time for the Malabar Coast, where the Arabian Sea laps lazily.

Editor's tip: Don't be put off by monsoon season (June-October). The rains are often brief, the beaches are empty and hotel rates are low.

Tamba, Japan

It's called *hotaru gassen* —the battle of the fireflies —when great masses of glittering pinpricks rise from the river valleys of Tamba, creating a luminescence to rival the starry sky's. In neon-lit Japan, the light-sensitive fireflies only appear in the darkest areas, so this small rural region in Hyōgo Prefecture, 60km north of Kōbe, is one of the last strongholds. Here, the Asian firefly performs its annual mating ritual, the final chapter in its life (it is the females of the species that flicker, at a rate of more than 150 times a minute, creating a strobe-like effect). Their appearance marks the start of the hot, humid Japanese summer.

Editor's tip: Late June and throughout July is peak season for Tamba's fireflies. Arrive just before dusk, as the show begins shortly after sunset, peaking 60 minutes later and slowing until around midnight. Calm, moonless nights are best.

Chicago, USA

At 400m up, Chicago's urban sprawl appears like a city-sized circuit board, coursing with current. This is the view from The Ledge at Skydeck, a quartet of glass boxes bolted like swallows' nests onto the side of the Willis Tower, the dual-pronged 'TV remote'-shaped building that rules the city's skyline. But to get a real sense of Chicago's energy, you have to get down to street level: from the din of the elevated 'L' trains that rattle around the central Loop district, to the honk of taxis dropping shoppers along the Magnificent Mile (or the shrieks of skaters swirling around Millennium Park's ice rink at Christmas)... America's third-largest city is a perpetual dynamo.

Editor's tip: For the best city views, arrive 30-45 minutes before sunset, to watch it sink beyond the horizon (theskydeck.com). And beware Chicago's freezing winters; the best time to travel is spring or autumn.

Alsace, France

Grab a bottle and a picnic blanket: you've found one of the prettiest — and fizziest — spots on the Alsace wine route. This half-timbered town in northeastern France is right in Riesling country (and it's home to 11 estates where you can buy bottles of the stuff), but it's also terrific for Crémant d'Alsace, the gorgeous sparkling wine that's like Champagne at half the price. Many of the surrounding wineries have B&B rooms among the vines, but it's worth stumbling into the centre too: miraculously undamaged by World War II, Riquewihr's cobbled streets still feel 16th-century, with facades in heraldic colours trimmed by narrow archways and criss-crossed turrets.

Editor's tip: Strasbourg is the nearest airport, but you'll find more frequent, cheaper flights to Basel, around 45 minutes' drive away in Switzerland (the airport has a separate French sector, so you only need clear Customs once).

Chefchaouen, Morocco

Little wonder the city of Chefchaouen, largely untroubled by western tourists, is nicknamed Morocco's 'Blue Pearl'. Its medina is the colour of forget-me-nots, its distant horizon a swathe of Matisse-hued Mediterranean Sea. Teetering between two peaks (*chaoua* means 'horns') in the Rif mountains, the city is a bewitching tangle of side streets and spiralling stairwells that funnel scents of cardamom and cloves, as the smell of dried roses mingles with cedarwood smoke from back-alley workshops.

Editor's tip: Chefchaouen, in its bed of lush greenery 600m above sea level, is a corner of Morocco you can visit even in high summer. While Marrakech bakes in temperatures of up to 35°C in July, the city maintains a spring-like 23°C. Want to join the locals? Take a picnic to the always-cool Ras-el-Maa waterfall on the edge of town.

Calabria, Italy

Right in Italy's toe — where rubble-strewn mountains sprout like bunions and craggy coves blister the sun-baked coast – is a region still shady with mafia and black-veiled widows. Calabria's base charm is unreconstructed and wild — a world away from Capri's chichi appeal or Portofino's polished elegance. Inland, three lesser-visited national parks soar to the clouds, hiding wild boar, bears and rare birds as well as tumbling waterfalls and lakes coloured deep green by the surrounding forests. But it's the beaches that make this a must-do: long, deserted sweeps of vanilla sand, where Ionian waves whisper of Greece across the water.

Editor's tip: Consider a two-centre trip, as this region is vast — a trip from the beach to the mountains can take more than two hours.

Berlin, Germany

How's this for a party? Around one million people turn up to usher in the New Year on the two-kilometre stretch between Berlin's Brandenburg Gate (pictured) and Victory Column — that's four times more than in London. They come for a firework extravaganza, food stalls with grub from across the globe, post-midnight party tents with star DJs, and live performances featuring everyone from Jermaine Jackson to Katherine Jenkins — and, of course, Germany's adopted son, David Hasselhoff, who wowed the crowds back in 2013. There are no tickets: just arrive before they shut the gates (usually around 9pm), and prepare for a long wait and a tight squeeze...

Editor's tip: Turning up with lots of booze will get you barred. The allowance is half a (plastic) bottle per person, but you can buy beer on site. This *is* Germany, after all.

To-Sua Ocean Trench, Upolu, Samoa

Swimming is big in Samoa (along with rugby, comparing tattoos, going to church, and racing *fautasi*, the local 45-man canoes). The spirited South Pacific nation, four hours' flight north of New Zealand, stages international swimming festivals and contests year-round, and cooling dunks under thundering waterfalls are a national pastime, as are dips in swimming holes. Among the most loved is this one on the southeast coast of Upolu, Samoa's gateway island. Padding down a long, wooden stairway, you emerge in an enchanted grotto of glossy foliage overhanging a bowl of clear water. To be christened an honorary local, all you need to do is dive in...

Editor's tip: Expect jet lag *and* head spin. Due to Samoa's position just over the date line, your 30-odd-hour flight there will appear to take two days — but only 20 hours coming back.

Empire State Building, New York

Wind-whipped hair and sparkling eyes — enlivened by the air that swirls around the Empire State Building's outdoor viewing deck — infuse your skyline selfie with some of the city's razzamatazz: its jazz-club snare, its restaurant clatter, its traffic honk. Sure, New York has topped this tower's height in recent years, but the Empire State remains the original and best. Downtown, the One World Observatory has a corporate gloss and theme-park-feel that undermines the mere 12m it has on its uptown rival. Here, at ESB, Manhattan's golden era lives on, as you queue along red carpet and past velvet ropes snaking to Art Deco lifts, with gentlemanly, waistcoated porters to guide you.

Editor's tip: Want that *Sleepless in Seattle* panorama by night? It's yours — often *all* yours, on a quiet weeknight — as the place is open til 2am.

Lake Baikal, Russia

If this is how you imagine Siberia... you're right. Lake Baikal sits high in that icy region's mountains, on the borders of the land once known as Outer Mongolia. But the enchantment isn't just in the names: this is the largest, deepest expanse of freshwater in the world — 25 million years old, and holding the same volume of water as all of America's Great Lakes put together. Even more magical, it's home to an array of bizarre species not found anywhere else on the planet: you might spot the Russian Desman (like a cross between an otter and a vole), the chubby, earless Nerpa (the world's only freshwater seal), or the Baikal Oilfish, a prehistoric-looking, translucent fish without scales — that gives birth to around 1,000 babies at a time.

Editor's tip: The ice may look enticing, but Siberian winter temperatures can dip to −40°C. Better to go in summer, when you can hike along 100km of lake shore on the Frolikha Adventure Coastline Track.

Vanuatu, South Pacific

Cut adrift 1,000km west of Fiji, the 83 islands of Vanuatu are a coconut-scented, beach-fringed Bali Hai (no coincidence James Michener, whose books inspired the musical, *South Pacific*, was stationed here during the War). Ringed by coral reef, the islands offer spectacular snorkelling and diving (the SS President Coolidge, sunk in WWII, is the largest wreck dive in the world), while boutique beach resorts — as opposed to high-rise hotels — are, thankfully, the norm here. Slow-paced and traditional, the islands are among the friendliest in Melanesia — village *kava* bars are a hoot, with coconut crab curry the ultimate hangover cure.

Editor's tip: Largest island Espiritu Santo is riddled with cobalt Blue Holes. Riri Blue Hole is one of the quietest and clearest (that's 20 minutes' cycle from Luganville, then 30 jungly minutes by canoe).

West Lake, Hangzhou, China

What a picture: pagodas, pine trees, morning mist over a mauve-tinted lake trailed by willows and a thousand layers of green... Small wonder China's greatest artists, poets and writers have been moved for nearly two millennia by the West Lake, in Hangzhou, 45 minutes by high-speed train from Shanghai. Every season shocks anew — hot-pink lotus flowers in summer, maples red and gold in autumn, plum trees speckled with snowflakes in winter — but the lake is at its best in spring, as cherry blossom and Yulan magnolias burst into bloom, scenting the air. Take a traditional *sampan* boat out on the early morning waters and you'll see it all at its dewy best.

Editor's tip: Hangzhou's many cycle paths are a blur of bright-red bicycles, which you can hire for 50p a day. Circle the lake and you'll pass tea houses and go over ornamental bridges.

Monti Sibillini National Park, Italy

Straddling the mountainous northern regions of Marche and Umbria is a landscape of granite peaks and cloud-kissed plateaux. It's wild, remote and sparsely inhabited, but once a year it plays host to a camera-defying festival of colour. Triggered by a glut of sunlight, rashes of violets, poppies and flowering lentils spread across the rolling hills, colouring the landscape with swatches of pink, yellow and blue. Get a better look by following one of the paths along the field borders, across the valley floor — with flowers rippling in all directions, you may find yourself breaking into something from *The Sound of Music*.

Editor's tip: The big bloom takes place from late May through to mid-June, making a scenic drive through the national park all the more ravishing. Fairytale Castelluccio di Norcia is the nearest town.

Machu Picchu, Peru

It's one of the most recognisable relics in the world, a UNESCO-protected, 15th-century city high in the clouds. Machu Picchu's Inca beauty and breath-catching Andes views have made it a must-do on millions of bucket lists, so you'll need planning to make a visit memorable for the right reasons. Avoid altitude sickness (Machu Picchu is 2,430m above sea level) with a couple of acclimatising days in the nearest town, Aguas Calientes. Starting here will also get you to the ruins long before the 11am coach-trip rush. Book a private guide and ask them to go in the opposite direction to the tour groups; that way you'll also avoid the crowds in front of the site's monuments.

Editor's tip: This holiday is best booked with a specialist travel company, who will use reliable guides and organise tickets in advance (try Journey Latin America, for example; journeylatinamerica.co.uk).

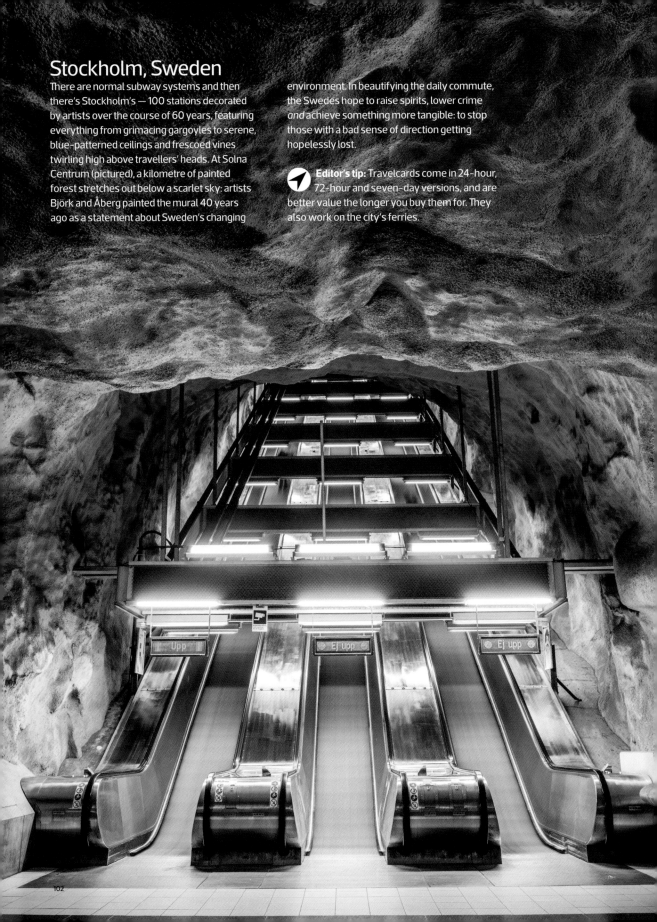

Stockholm, Sweden

There are normal subway systems and then there's Stockholm's — 100 stations decorated by artists over the course of 60 years, featuring everything from grimacing gargoyles to serene, blue-patterned ceilings and frescoed vines twirling high above travellers' heads. At Solna Centrum (pictured), a kilometre of painted forest stretches out below a scarlet sky: artists Björk and Åberg painted the mural 40 years ago as a statement about Sweden's changing environment. In beautifying the daily commute, the Swedes hope to raise spirits, lower crime *and* achieve something more tangible: to stop those with a bad sense of direction getting hopelessly lost.

Editor's tip: Travelcards come in 24-hour, 72-hour and seven-day versions, and are better value the longer you buy them for. They also work on the city's ferries.

Pointe d'Esny, Mauritius

The picture of peaceful, sleepy, Indian Ocean indolence? Not *beneath* the waves, it isn't, mate. What look like tiny, lapping ripples to us humans are huge swells to the underwater citizens of the Mauritian coast, tumbling and churning with the trade winds near the southern town of Mahébourg. A metre or two down, there's even more hubbub — Mauritius is haloed by the world's third-largest reef, creating a band of natural lagoons best explored with a snorkel or glass-bottomed boat. Stripey orange clownfish, neon-blue surgeonfish and spiky firefish dart between the bronze-red coral and curly anemones. But as you bob about with the marine life, do glimpse back at the coast: guava and scarlet-dotted flamboyant trees (that's their actual name!) nodding on the shoreline, sugarcane fields shimmying across the ridge of extinct volcanoes... and all framed by a royal-blue sky.

Editor's tip: Nearby Mahébourg is the dock for daily boat trips to teeny coral Île aux Aigrettes — an island nature reserve, and home of the rare pink pigeon and giant tortoise.

Steptoe Butte State Park, Washington, USA

Sprayed in late-summer golden sunlight, Washington State's ivy-green Palouse Hills take on an otherworldly quality — a rippling Sahara dotted with isolated grain silos and shadowy stands of Douglas fir. Draped over the southeastern corner of Washington, as well as parts of northwestern Idaho and northern Oregon, this crumpled quilt of a landscape was once nothing but native prairie, kept lawn-short by roaming herds of buffalo. Now, covered in fields of wheat and flowering lentils, the area is largely farmland, though no less magical. It's also a pocket of pure Americana, with the nearby brown-brick frontier towns of Colfax and Palouse dotted with retro motels, honky-tonk cowboy bars and cute Victorian clapboard houses.

Editor's tip: For the ultimate 360° panorama, drive your hire car to the top of Steptoe Butte, a standalone cone of rock that has views of the entire surrounding landscape.

St Mary, Jamaica

Coconuts and bananas, guava and plantains, limes and a bright smile — could *you* resist pulling over? This is a corner of Jamaica that's colourful for plenty of other reasons, too. Over the years, a truly glamorous cast has passed through St Mary Parish, a mountainous, green chunk of the north coast that lies east of the Ocho Rios tourist heartland. Beside the sea at Oracabessa is Ian Fleming's old house, Goldeneye, where he wrote his 007 novels. Today it's a luxury resort owned by Chris 'Island Records' Blackwell: waves lap James Bond Beach, where scenes from *Dr No* were shot, and Rihanna and Lauryn Hill now perform. And one of Fleming's guests was Noël Coward — who, smitten, built his own house nearby (then added another). Now his first one, Blue Harbour is also a hotel; the other, Firefly, a national monument to the playwright. Come to see his piano, desk and grave — and Jamaica's finest coastal views.

Editor's tip: Want *double* glamour? Pick Villa Chica at Coward's former digs, Blue Harbour: you'll be staying in the same Art Deco cottage as Marlene Dietrich and Katharine Hepburn did.

105

Singapore

Part space-age metropolis, part window into Asia's ancient cultures, this seaside city-state makes a great getaway. That bit of water on the left is the world's largest infinity pool — perfect for a warm wallow as you gaze down at the 'scraper-filled skyline from the 57th floor of Marina Bay Sands hotel. Or you could stroll the OCBC Skyway at dusk, wandering 22m above ground between gigantic, tree-like sculptures adorned with tightly-packed plants. But as well as these billion-dollar, brand-new attractions, there are captivating old corners ripe for discovery. Chinatown and Little India both deserve a day: the former comes with ornate shophouses, hectic food courts and street markets packed with souvenirs, while the latter has multicoloured temples, fortune-telling parakeets, and the smell of jasmine seeping from the streetside flower stalls.

Editor's tip: You might think it tastes like cough syrup, but you can't leave without drinking a Singapore Sling; Raffles hotel serves the original gin-based cocktail.

Kakku Pagodas, Myanmar

An elegant symbol of the devotion of the local Pa-O people, the 2,500 Buddhist stupas at Kakku are tightly — and a little surreally — packed into just a one-kilometre clearing. The structures span two millennia (though most are around 300 years old) and, while some are starkly simple, others come decorated with carvings of dragons, musicians and dancers, or intricate floral patterns. Many are still topped with their original umbrella-like, metal structures, adorned with bells that fill the air with tinkling melodies. And though over-restoration has taken away some of the site's magic, the stupas remain toweringly impressive, standing protective over the deserted countryside two hours west of temple-trimmed Inle Lake. Here, as if more magic were required, floating gardens and markets bob in the shadows of two mist-topped mountain ranges.

Editor's tip: Travel using internal flights or with a large, well-respected tour operator, as there can be conflict in Myanmar, and the roads are badly maintained (try, for instance, Steppes Travel; steppestravel.co.uk).

Morondava, Madagascar

Everything on this unearthly Indian Ocean island pulsates with strangeness — including a language that could drive a computer spell-checker to despair (one famous king was called Andriantsimitoviaminandriandehibe). Then there are the trees: there are six species of baobab on Madagascar (Grandidier's is the largest) — they take centuries to grow 30m tall and achieve a Sumo-worthy girth of 7.5m. Sunrise and sunset are the best times to admire this captivating parade of gentle giants near Morondava on the island's west coast. Here, they stretch for four kilometres — a nice, long stroll, while contemplating the slow burn of nature in one of the most exotic countries on the planet.

Editor's tip: Our summer is the dry season, when the weather is cool, the baobabs are in flower, and it's easy to travel around (for the rest of the year it's Muddygascar). Finish up with some R&R on the beautiful, beach-rimmed island of Boraha (also known as Île Sainte-Marie) — August is a great month for whale-watching there.

Steakhouse, Buenos Aires

It has a vocab all of its own: *lomo, vacio, entraña, costeleta, asado*. Buenos Aires' steak scene doesn't do things by halves — as evidenced by the 12 or so different cuts of beef on your *parrilla* (steakhouse) menu, costing from just £6, and the salivating diners clamouring to choose. First-timer? Order the *bife de chorizo* (sometimes *bife angosto*) — a distant cousin of the juicy sirloin, served fatty and rich with the omnipresent, peppery *chimichurri* sauce for which this steak capital is so famous. As for sides, the true Argentinian way is meat on meat — but a grilled corn on the cob or a potato salad won't get you laughed out of the joint.

Editor's tip: Palermo and San Telmo neighbourhoods are both great steak-hunting grounds, with a selection of swanky spots and down-home *bodegóns*. Or consider a walking tour around a few (try parrillatour.com).

Lac Blanc, Chamonix, France

Winter in the Alps isn't just about piste-bashing. Take a cable car up over the Chamonix Valley for a dizzying panorama of the Massif du Mont Blanc. This stretch of Western Europe's mightiest mountain range is home to Mont Blanc, at 4,810m its highest peak. You'll get a front-row view from Lac Blanc, 2,350m up, where a hiking trail reaches the cafe. In summer, you can walk (five hours) up through pine forests from Col des Montets; in winter, you can do it in half the time, by taking a cable car from the village of Les Praz. Hop out at Flégère, then crunch up through the snow (one hour 45 minutes) to reach the lake. Here you can gaze out to the Mer de Glace glacier as well as the razor-sharp ridge of the Chamonix Needles.

Editor's tip: In spring you don't even need to look up to take in the view — the frozen lake is like a giant mirror reflecting the Massif's meringue peaks.

El Nido, Philippines

Still scarred from a traumatically cold morning's kayaking with your Scout troop or on a school trip? El Nido's Bacuit Bay may be just what's required to get you back in that saddle. Deserted islets, pristine reef beneath a glowing green sea... this is arguably the pleasantest kayaking in the world. Hop between the bay's 22 uninhabited dollops of palmy green just off the northwestern tip of Palawan island and you'll be paddling through clingfilm-calm lagoons and beneath soaring limestone gorges — towards secret, Bounty-ad beaches. Pack your snorkelling gear and you can dive off into an underwater world of fluoro coral, damselfish, parrotfish and dancing seahorses, too.

Editor's tip: Though you can tour the islands independently, opting for an initial guided kayak trip will familiarise you with the conditions and geography. El Nido art cafe serves as the town's buzzy social centre and can organise kayak, hiking tours and scuba dives (elnidoboutiqueandartcafe.com).

Seattle, USA

The sky-kissing Space Needle is a part of Seattle forever cemented in a 1962 freeze-frame, when construction on this *War of the Worlds* tripod lookalike finished — and the crowds in town for that year's World's Fair soared to the heavens for breath-snatching views of Mount Rainier and the silvery sheet of Puget Sound. But down at ground level, Seattle's appeal is as dizzy as the view from atop the observation tower. Gleaming cut-outs of concrete and steel dominate the business district, while Pike Place Fish Market buzzes. (Don't miss the stall where white-coated fishmongers belt out *a cappella* numbers as they pick crabs and salmon for shoppers.)

Editor's tip: Pine Box bar (pineboxbar.com), up on Capitol Hill, used to serve as a funeral home, and was where martial-arts legend Bruce Lee was laid out. Might sound morbid, but it's now one of the best beer bars in town.

Port Quin Bay, Cornwall

In summer, the finger-shaped inlet that forms Port Quin — a cluster of stone cottages and a car park on the clotted-cream splodge that is North Cornwall's beautiful coast — drains to leave a playground of rock pools. After filling your bucket with starfish and shrimps, follow the South West Coast Path for three kilometres of blue sea views (look out for dolphins and basking sharks) all the way to pretty Port Isaac. Drop in for a crab sarnie at fish-shop-cum-cafe Fresh from the Sea, and a pint of Cornish Ale at The Golden Lion pub before the return walk to Port Quin.

Editor's tip: Push on round the coast from Port Isaac and you'll find idyllic Port Gaverne: a sandy cove with paddle-perfect waters. The easiest way to get here is by train into Newquay station, where Cornwall Car Hire can meet you (newquaycarhire.co.uk).

Ganesh Visarjan Festival, Mumbai

Every city gets the gods it deserves. In go-getting Mumbai, residents reserve their devotions for Lakshmi, the Hindu goddess of wealth (depicted bedecked in mobile phones), and Ganesh, the elephant-headed deity often said to remove all obstacles to worldly success. Ganesh Visarjan, 'the immersion of Ganesh', is the apex of the Indian city's annual 10-day elephant-god festival, when a million-plus Mumbaikars descend on the city's Girgaum beach. They come weaving in procession behind giant effigies, soundtracked by a riot of firecrackers, cymbals and drums, before ritually, deliriously dunking the jug-eared one in the Arabian Sea.

Editor's tip: The festival takes place around August/September — great timing to avoid both the monsoons and peak tourist period. The full 10-day affair is known as Ganesh Chaturthi.

Hoher Kasten, Switzerland

The hills are alive – with Swiss hikers, from May to September. And with vistas like this one, which takes in the Appenzell Alps from 1,795m up, it's easy to see why rambling is the nation's favourite pastime. Go native by pulling on boots and following the neatly marked trails that set off from Hoher Kasten's summit, but don't forget the supermarket *wurst* (the Swiss can barbecue anywhere, and there are communal grills scattered about the landscape). Or cheat, and take the cable car to the revolving restaurant atop the mountain: you'll take in views of six countries from the comfort of your gently circling seat.

Editor's tip: Visitors often combine Hoher Kasten with a stay in pricey Zürich, but the pretty German border town of Konstanz makes for a significantly cheaper break, as well as a shorter journey time to the mountain.

Borobudur, Indonesia

On some days, the clouds overhanging Central Java's rainforests obstruct this fiery sunrise. But when conditions are right at 1,200-year-old Borobudur, this enormous Buddhist temple and its 72 lava-stone stupas appear to glow like gold. Constructed from two million stone blocks, and stretching 35m high, this elaborate structure outside Yogyakarta city dwarfs most other Southeast Asian temples in both scale and majesty. Up close, it dazzles with its thousands of carved reliefs and Buddha statues, some so perfectly detailed they look like they were hewn yesterday. Start at the top of the layer-cake-like structure, where you can take in the surrounding countryside, then work your way down.

Editor's tip: Avoid Christmas and mid-June to mid-July, when local visitors descend on the site. And book into the Manohara Hotel —it's the only accommodation on Borobudur's grounds — so you can enter 90 minutes before the usual 6am opening time and get *that* sunrise to yourself.

Ponta Grossa, Ceará, Brazil

Where, you might be wondering, are the crowds? Answer: they're on Rio's Copacabana. And the delicious deserted beaches lining the 600km coast of Ceará state, in Brazil's tropical northeast, are as far from the frenetic sands of Rio as is possible — as laid-back as a lullaby, as calming as a Caipirinha sipped in a swinging hammock in the shade of coconut palms. No 'strutting your stuff', then, and no irritatingly beautiful bodies to block views of the glassy Atlantic waves. A stay here is about pacing kilometres of empty, pepper-fine sand and stopping for spicy tiger prawns cooked at some tiny shack. Day done, fishermen return in their boats, billowing sails golden in the low, late-afternoon light, weighed down with more sea treats, fresh for your delectation.

Editor's tip: Few visitors know this, but some of the most spectacular Atlantic views are yours on a walk through the sand dunes east of Ponta Grossa village. And visit Brazil in November — leave it any later and prices rocket as Christmas and Carnival (around February) approach.

Havana, Cuba

There's no such thing as a quiet stroll in Cuba's capital. The once splendid colonial streets sing with chatter, street sellers and the chug of patched-up vintage Chevrolets. Music seeps from bars, and bicycle taxis tout for business with a clatter of bells. And, though many modern Cubans opt for a uniform of tight jeans and even tighter tops, the ruffly Bata Cubana dress still gets an airing in the crumbling Old Town, where women pose for pictures in their own cloud of giggling banter. Cigars, however, are falling out of favour. Smoked long before Christopher Columbus washed up here in 1492, they're slowly being outlawed in bars and restaurants.

Editor's tip: Of the Havana cigar factories, El Laguito — set in a creamy mansion among greenery — is the prettiest. Ask a concierge or fixer to organise: it's not officially open to the public. (Front desk staff usually know somebody — or somebody who knows somebody — to fix up most experiences, from watching baseball to ballet, to riding in a 1950s Buick.)

Uluru, Australia

Rising from the plains at the parched centre of Australia, 600-million-year old Uluru stands more than 800m above the Outback plains, shimmering like a solitary, ochre mirage. Formerly known as Ayers Rock, the sacred sandstone was returned to Aboriginal owners in 1985, since when tourists have been discouraged from climbing on it. Sunset selfies, on the other hand, are all the rage: just make sure you hang around 15 minutes after sundown, when the rock blazes brightest. Book a campfire BBQ for mighty views of the night sky.

Editor's tip: Uluru steals the headlines, but the three-hour Valley of the Wind hike through nearby Kata Tjuta (an eerie dreamscape of 36 mini-Ulurus formerly known as The Olgas) is one that no adventurer should miss.

Bodiam Castle, East Sussex, UK

Bodiam is so sand-castle perfect you almost expect to find a super-size bucket and spade discarded nearby, and a giant older brother threatening to kick it over. It wouldn't take much strength, either — the castle looks sturdy, but it's actually quite weak. Supposedly built to stave off French pirates, it ended up as a showpiece 'fortification' with wine cellars, servants' quarters and lovely lodgings for its owner — but walls so thin they'd crumble at the sound of gunshot. Fortunately, it managed to avoid bombardment for 600 years; and by the 18th century, it was a romantic ivy-clad ruin. Then, in the early 1900s, Lord Curzon visited and fell in love with Bodiam, so he bought and restored it — the castle's very own knight in shining armour.

Editor's tip: Recognise Bodiam, but can't quite place it? The property has played the part of 'British Castle' in umpteen Arthurian films, including *Monty Python and the Holy Grail*.

Oruro Carnival, Bolivia

While Rio roasts, a cool alternative Mardi Gras is taking place in Brazil's neighbour, Bolivia. High in the Andes, in one neon-bright blowout before Lent begins, 30,000 revellers shimmy through the streets of the mountaintop city of Oruro. Some are dressed as fierce Inca gods, in bird-of-paradise feather headdresses; others form dance troupes, bedecked with silver bells; and the carnival climaxes with the Diablada dance, where glittering archangels battle devils in garish masks, bristling with teeth and tusks. It all begins on the Saturday before Ash Wednesday, in February or March — and the *chicha* (fermented-corn booze) flows freely among the partiers who pack the city for a full 10 days.

Editor's tip: Acclimatise — heady Oruro is 3,700m above sea level. Spend a couple of days doing nothing, and drink plenty of Coca tea.

Tunnel of Love, Ukraine

It looks like the work of an 18th-century landscape architect for some spendthrift aristocrat. A clue to its far more workaday use lies in the tracks you can just make out running through the 'Tunnel of Love', in northwest Ukraine. These arching trees form a stretch of railway route for deliveries of birch to the Odek plywood factory: founded in the late 19th century at the end of the 6.5km line, it is still in business. The finished goods are dispatched back, the same way, to the terminus at Klevan, and from there, ultimately, to companies across Western Europe. Thanks to ongoing demand, the trains run several times daily, and continue to shape the foliage to this day.

Editor's tip: In September and October, the Tunnel is ablaze with autumn colours — best visited as part of a private tour from the capital, Kiev (ukraine-kiev-tour.com).

South Beach, Miami

Squeezed up together along Miami's Ocean Drive, the iconic hotels of South Beach seem almost edible – like giant Mr Kipling French Fancies with their pastel-icing coats, nibble-worthy Art Deco ornamentation and Streamline Moderne curves apparently piped on by a *pâtissier*. They're so much part of the city's image it's hard to imagine that, as the 20th century wore on, they were destined for demolition — tawdry vestiges of a vanished era. Appalled by the threat of their imminent annihilation, in 1976, Deco-obsessive Barbara Baer Capitman helped found the Miami Design Preservation League (mdpl.org) — without her, a fair few sexy fashion advertisements and MTV videos would never have shimmied into existence.

Editor's tip: This stretch is down near the southern end, where the best people-watching can be had. Be sure to observe the dress code: skimpy.

Budapest, Hungary

Like a super-sized slab of *gâteau*, the Hungarian Parliament Building dominates the east bank of the Danube in Budapest. It's a visual banquet in itself, but is really just the icing on the cake when it comes to the city's architectural heritage. Just a short walk away, for instance, is Neo-Renaissance St Stephen's Basilica with its twin bell towers.Once you've absorbed its Fabergé interiors, take the lift (or 364 stairs) to the top of the dome for 360° views. Reward yourself afterwards with a rose-shaped ice cream from next-door Gelarto Rosa, then round things off with a visit to the Baroque Széchenyi Baths, to watch venerable-looking bearded types play chess wreathed with steam — or join the couples wallowing in the soothing waters.

Editor's tip: Buildings that were left to decay during Soviet rule have been given a new lease of life as hip 'ruin' bars. The Szimpla Kert (szimpla.hu) is the original and best.

Myrtos Beach, Kefallonia

It's a sunny morning on the island made famous by *Captain Corelli's Mandolin*. As you come over the brow of the hill, Myrtos unfurls. The waters are transparent; the shore, freckled with parasols, bright in the sunshine. Flanked by high white cliffs — *kimilia* — at each end, it is one of those rare finds, a beach even more arresting than it appears in pictures. Because it's never been settled — there's no village, no resort — it has remained virginal. And since the only way you can get here is by car, even in summer it feels uncrowded. There's a single beach bar, a few neat rows of sunloungers, that preternaturally blue sea... and nothing else.

Editor's tip: The beach bar is overpriced, so hop back in the car and head for the village of Divarata, a couple of kilometres away. Hunker down for a lunch of fresh grilled sardines and Greek salad at Alexandros.

Salzburg, Austria

What a showstopper! Like the city-sized set of some grand opera, Salzburg's skyline fills the air with drama. Baroque spires and domes raise the roof between rainbow-petalled gardens and toy-town squares, all conducted regally from on high by the Hohensalzburg Fortress. The city has music in the air: it gave the world Mozart and set the scene for *The Sound of Music* film. Summer ups the tempo with a top-notch classical-music festival, and warms the squares and parks where string quartets and buskers play. Ferdinand-Hanusch-Platz and Mozartplatz are two of the most tuneful, but step inside for church recitals and concert dinners.

Editor's tip: To hear the purest notes in the city's musical calendar, attend summer's Salzburg Festival. But if opera tickets are too pricey, head out to Kapitelplatz in the evenings, where small concerts and screenings are free to all.

Coimbra, Portugal

Nowhere does packaging like Portugal. Shopping-list items as prosaic as soap and tinned fish are transmogrified into covetable souvenirs thanks to display-me designs on their paper wrappings. And nothing gets the Portuguese packaging treatment like its buildings: churches, palaces, railway stations and houses are clad in decorative tiles — *azulejos* — bearing geometric designs, historic tableaux, and sometimes a cheeky cherub. One of the most head-spinning examples of the art can be seen in Coimbra, Portugal's former capital, in the chapel of the 700-year-old university. Tiles run floor to ceiling, in intricate patterns of that effortlessly evocative blue, yellow and white.

Editor's tip: You'll see plenty of *azulejos* without even leaving the cities — the Jerónimos monastery in Lisbon has some fine friezes, as does the entrance hall of Porto's main train station.

Eiffel Tower, Paris

So derided was engineer Eiffel's 'Dame de Fer' before completion in 1889, there was every chance it might not survive until the next century, let alone make it into the Millennium and beyond, a totem to grit and glamour. Famous names, from Guy de Maupassant to Charles Gounod, spoke out against the plans, lambasting the prospect of a 'truly tragic street lamp' and 'giant ungainly skeleton'. But Eiffel shrugged off the criticism, and his baby proceeded to attract 400,000 visitors the following year. Except during the two world wars, when it was shuttered, the iron-filigree icon has drawn tourists like bees to honey ever since, with numbers now exceeding six million a year. Royalty have made the ascent, as have stars, political luminaries and even an elephant — each helping secure that elegant Tower's own celebrity.

Editor's tip: The last lift is at 10.30pm (11pm in summer). Not only are queues far shorter than during the day, the view is more dramatic with the city lit by night — particularly in iffy weather.

Moon Hill, Yangshuo, China

Looming hundreds of metres above a sea of greenery in the county of Yangshuo, southeast China, is a sight so perfectly formed, it might have been computer-generated. The arch is what's left of a hollow peak, once a highlight of the local karst topography, but long since collapsed — up close you can see the wand-like stalactites hanging from the old cave roof. That odd name, Moon Hill, starts to make sense as you approach, ascending the 800 steps to the base: the closer you get, the smaller the aperture shrinks, framing the moon as it fades from the evening sky, the way an aspirin dissolves in a glass of water.

Editor's tip: Visit during our autumn and you'll miss the tourist hordes and sweltering humidity, arriving just in time for sunshine, clear blue skies and comfy temperatures — ideal for exploring. For a taste of rural China, rent a bike (about £8 a day) from a vendor on West Street, in the nearby town of Yangshuo, and make the seven-kilometre ride to Moon Hill through jungle and pretty, tumbledown villages.

Grenada, Caribbean

This little guy is already a survivor. Making it into the sea from the sandy nest where he was born just minutes earlier, the green turtle has dodged the crabs and gulls who had so many of his just-hatched siblings for dinner. If his luck holds, he could live to see his 80th birthday — and to improve his chances, he's going to head for deep waters until he's a bit bigger, which is why it's a rare treat to see a young green turtle in the water. Rare, but not impossible — and in the waters around Grenada, the lush Caribbean island renowned for its nutmeg and cinnamon, you may get lucky yourself. (If not, there's always leatherback, loggerhead and hawksbill turtles to look out for, among the seahorses and those pretty grey angelfish…)

Editor's tip: Levera Beach, in northeast Grenada, is a major nesting sight for leatherback turtles — come April-July for the best chance of seeing the females nesting, and the babies hatching.

Brussels, Belgium

You can leave your diet at home when you set off for Brussels. The Belgian capital, famous for its chocolate, beer and mayo-slathered chips, is no place for leaf-munching restraint, whatever you think of its sprouts. Besides, there are the waffles. Two types of waffle, in fact: Brussels (lighter, squarer, with deeper dimples), and Liège (denser, chewier, sweeter). Mostly, waffles are street food: trucks sell them wrapped in paper, to be wolfed down on the spot. But sometimes, especially when you've been hoofing it round the sights — the Manneken Pis fountain and the Grand Place's baroque guildhouses, say — you just need to sit down. Try Maison Dandoy; the company better known for its spicy *speculoos* biscuits promises to 'make your senses twinkle and dance', and in its tearoom on Rue Charles Buls, it does just that.

Editor's tip: Our favourite waffle (*gaufre*) is served at the Chalet Robinson cafe in Cambre Woods — where British soldiers played cricket the day before the battle of Waterloo. You can pedal a Villo city bike here in just 20 minutes.

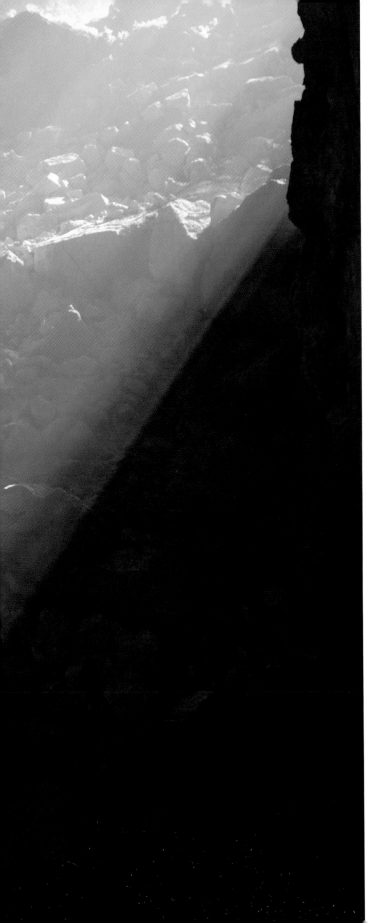

Hang En Cave, Vietnam

Hidden beneath a swathe of tropical rainforest, it's a setting to send the imagination into overdrive: a cathedral of a natural cavern, sunlight knifing through the gloom, illuminating boulders the size of houses. A 10-hour drive from Hanoi, in central Vietnam's Phong Nha-Ke-Bang National Park, you'd never find the world's third-largest cave without a guide — but you won't forget it once you've camped the night by that pool, listening for the chirrup of langur monkeys or the kerfuffle of flying foxes bundling in to shelter from the rain. Tours run between December and late August — access is too dangerous during the flood-prone rainy season — and Oxalis (oxalis.com.vn) is the most highly-rated operator.

Editor's tip: Weary feet? Dip them in the underground river for a free pedicure — the waters flowing through Phong Nha-Ke-Bang National Park are home to more than 170 species of fish, and smaller varieties are happy to nibble off any dry skin.

Pyhä Lake, Finland

You won't see many people by this lake during autumn. At the very edge of the Arctic Circle, Pyhä gets almost all its visitors when the snow starts to fall and skiers hit its slopes. More fool them: it's actually in September that this colour-wheel spectacle occurs. The Pyhä-Luosto National Park that surrounds the lake becomes a patchwork of green and gold, set against huge Scandinavian skies alive with puffing clouds. The Sami forest people who once lived here believed the area was filled with spirits. See if you can spot one on hikes through stream-etched forest, beside hidden waterfalls, and into dramatic ravines.

Editor's tip: Be prepared for 'traditional' (ahem, basic) Finnish life in this rural spot. You'll need to order alcoholic drinks in advance at the supermarket (they're not readily available in shops), and get cashback with your purchases as there's no ATM.

The Cook Islands

Brushed with ostrich-feather clouds, a pale blue sky unfurls toward the horizon. Below, as if pinned to a sash of turquoise sequins, lies a verdant islet, as beautiful as an emerald brooch. You're looking at one of the Cook Islands — 15 outcrops that make up this small South Pacific archipelago, rampant with rainforest, ringed with mother-of-pearl beaches. In rare areas of deep water, black-lipped oysters horde their precious orbs, while in the shallow lagoons, schools of fluoro fish swarm through wrecks and reefs of coral. Paradise lost? It's just been hiding here the whole time...

Editor's tip: Despite their position slap-bang in the middle of the Pacific Ocean, the Cook Islands aren't that hard to get to — plenty of UK companies sell holidays there (try Turquoise for a start; turquoiseholidays.co.uk). Our summer-to-autumn is the best and driest time to visit.

Serengeti National Park, Tanzania

East Africans think of the wildebeest as a freak of nature, cobbled together by God using leftover parts: part cow, part goat, with the head of a locust and tail of a lion. But freak or not, they make an impressive sight stampeding in their millions across the savannah, a column of hooves and dust. And standing over two metres high, with a top speed of 65kph, this quarter-tonne of muscle and horn is a work of precision engineering, with an in-built GPS to navigate the 3,000km migration from Tanzania's northern grasslands to Kenya's Masai Mara. No-one knows what makes the wildebeest leave their calving grounds for pastures new — lightning? Air pressure? DNA? But one thing is clear: the sight is a wonder to behold.

Editor's tip: January is the start of the calving season in the Serengeti. Brace yourself for lots of tottering babies — and opportunist predators.

Procida, Italy

Remember *Il Postino*? The Italian movie where the only sight dreamier than Massimo Troisi's face was the fishing village where he romanced his girl? Well, that's Marina Corricella. A jigsaw puzzle of jewel-bright houses adorned with laundry-lines and balconies lush with flowers, it tumbles down to a calm bay dotted with fishing boats and nets spread out to dry in the sun. It's still the prettiest spot on the island of Procida, off the coast of Naples, and you'll not find a better location for a lazy fish lunch, with a salad of chilli-spiced lemons — the local speciality — picked from the groves that cloak the green, volcanic landscape. Procida has slipped under the radar for all but the most devoted Italophiles, so (unlike its neighbouring islands, Capri and Ischia) it doesn't attract the late-summer tourists tussling for the best beach lounger or trattoria table.

Editor's tip: On a blazing day, Procida's finest assets are its clear coves. Well hidden, they're best enjoyed from the deck of a traditional *gozzo*, which looks like a wooden bathtub and floats like a rubber duck. Hire one, with captain, from the many Marina Chiaiolella-based outfits.

Seljalandsfoss, Iceland

See that path disappearing into shadow around the centre of this picture? And the steps that vanish from view down by the bottom? Well, they meet. Behind the waterfall. And even in a country with a whole saga's worth of awesome cascades, that makes Seljalandsfoss unique. It's not hard to get to, either: you'll see and hear it — as bright as Freya's hair, as thunderous as Thor in his fury — from Route 1, the surprisingly quiet two-lane road that encircles Iceland. The walk itself is easy, too, though take a plastic bag for your camera because the spray soaks *everything* back there. When should you go? We like July in Iceland as it means 'midnight sun' and Seljalandsfoss is a spectacular place to experience it, as that milky-pale orb dips towards the western horizon, aligning with the cave mouth and painting the cliff-face gold.

Editor's tip: Break the drive at Stokkseyri, between Reykjavík and Seljalandsfoss — it's a fishing village, and home to a bizarre little museum of Icelandic ghosts (draugasetrid.is).

Provence, France

Breathe deeply and you can almost smell it: the essence of summer in Provence. From Avignon to the mountainous Italian border, great expanses of purple flowers appear daubed in feathery brushstrokes across fields and sunny hillsides. Coming from the Latin word *lavare*, meaning 'to wash', lavender has been farmed here since Roman times, to be made into everything from soaps to sorbet. It can be bought dried and bound by the bundle at farmers' markets in crumbling hilltop towns, or infused by bees into the local honey. But we think the best way to take it in is to drive, windows down (even better, rooftop down), along *Les Routes de la Lavande*, a network of roads that criss-cross the region. For the full effect, go in June, which marks the beginning of the lavender season: temperatures are mild, the fields are in bloom, and the majority of holiday-makers are yet to arrive.

Editor's tip: Visit the Musée de la Lavande (museedelalavande.com) in the tiny village of Coustellet; it has its own range of beauty products produced on site.

Harbin Snow and Ice Festival, China

Pack your thermals and prepare to party: every winter, in China's northeastern corner (where Siberian winds send the mercury plummeting below -30°C), an entire sub-zero wonderland is carved out of frozen blocks, attracting more than a million visitors. It looks placid by day, but when the sun goes down, this nippy Narnia transforms into a Vegas on ice: the lights go on, music blares and crowds come out to play. Among frosty sculptures of life-sized figures, pagodas, and temples, you'll see scaled-down recreations of iconic international landmarks — a version of Rome's Colosseum, say, or Reykjavík's Hallgrímskirkja Church — with precipitous steps, slithery ice slides and soaring turrets to scale, to help keep the cold at bay.

Editor's tip: Fireworks start the festival with a bang in late December, and the party runs until the end of February, when visitors can help smash the melting sculptures.

Brecon Beacons, Wales

It's a long way from home for these Shetland ponies. Not that they're lost — they've been haunting these Welsh hills for so long, they're part of the scenery. Indeed, come sun or snow over the Brecon Beacons, they'll be grazing atop this spectacular spot at Hay Bluff, in the eastern Black Mountains. You, too, will need an equine steadiness of step to find them — it's a steep climb up the path from the car park to the top, 677m above sea level. But as your gaze roams across the Wye Valley, the views will take the ache from your legs — as will the mane attraction.

Editor's tip: Only five places in the world have been granted 'international dark sky reserve status', and this is one of them. On a crisp, clear winter's night, star-gazers here can see the Milky Way, meteor showers and constellation after constellation.

Blue Hole, Belize

If it looks like the entrance to another world, that's probably because it is. Dive through the implacable surface of this jewel-like wonder and you'll find yourself among some truly alien-looking creatures, from unearthly-colourful parrotfish to Martian-eyed barracudas. Strap on scuba tank and fins, and it's easy to believe you're travelling in time, too: this eerie, watery wormhole hasn't changed since Jacques Cousteau first plumbed its abyss in 1971, confirming it as an ancient karst-limestone landscape submerged, Atlantis-like, by rising seas. There's even a glimpse of the last Ice Age, which created this curiosity: a drowned cave system of stalagmites, stalactites and eerily gothic cathedral-pipe columns. In-depth history indeed.

Editor's tip: The Blue Hole is a two-hour voyage from shore — often through rough seas — so pack travel-sickness tablets and eat light beforehand.

San Francisco, USA

It's enough to induce Summer of Love flashbacks, this psychedelic view of San Francisco's skyline. The effect is appropriate — this is Alamo Square, around the corner from the Haight-Ashbury district, aka hippie central, with its medical marijuana dispensaries, thrift stores and coffee shops leaking Beatles' tracks into the street. Take a stroll and you'll soon find the 'painted ladies' — Victorian houses that were jazzed-up in a palette of candy pastels in the 1960s. The most famous (pictured), slope down Steiner Street towards the Marina, backlit by the glittering skyscrapers of the city's Financial District.

Editor's tip: Spring is a great time to visit, and proves the hippie spirit is alive and well, with festivals bustin' out all over. The best is Carnaval (carnaval sanfrancisco.org), which transforms the Mexican-flavoured Mission District into a huge street party (May).

Zakynthos, Greece

There's only one way to get to and from Shipwreck Beach — as the hapless crew of this liner found out when they washed up here on a stormy night back in 1980. With no road or footpath access, the lovely lemon wedge of sand sees a lot of (more fortunate) boat trippers these days: it's a must-do for tourists, who come to swim in the electric blue water just offshore. But beyond the island's best-known bay, there are equally photogenic stretches waiting to be discovered. Seeking them out — along roads where traffic lights don't exist, and signs are scrawled on driftwood and obscured by burgeoning olive trees — is part of the adventure.

Editor's tip: Shipwreck Beach gets packed on summer days, so visit in May or September, or from 3pm onwards when most visitors head back to their hotels. Don't forget your parasol, either — the white surrounding cliffs reflect heat on to the beach, so it's searing at noon. The only other shade is cast by *The Panagiotis*, the shipwreck that gave this cove (aka Navagio Beach) its evocative name.

La Boca, Buenos Aires

Threaded through the down-at-heel *barrio* of La Boca, colourful alley El Caminito is worth hopping on the local bus for. Tree trunks wear psychedelic crocheted coats, and owl puppets catch your eye. Follow the tourist throng along it to La Bombonera (Diego Maradona's old home stadium), past patchwork-bright houses of concrete and clapboard, painted tangerine, cobalt, scarlet and peppermint by the Italian immigrants who once lived here. Tango murals come in every style, and if you're lucky you'll catch the real deal, performers strutting cheek-to-

cheek to a wheezing accordion (try La Barrica cafe). With the twisted faces of Che Guevara, Eva Peron and Pope puppets leering from balconies, there's something of the travelling funfair in La Boca — a touch of haunted house, wrapped in candy colours. Bring a few pesos to thank any street artists you take photos of (but nothing you can't afford to lose).

Editor's tip: La Boca is a neighbourhood to dip into, not linger in — foreigners are advised not to wander far from the station and El Caminito.

Antarctica

It's true: what you see here is just one tenth of this giant iceberg — the rest lies deep beneath those chilly waves. (Chilly to us, anyway; for these penguins it feels scorching — this shot was taken during the Antarctic summer (our winter), the only time it's possible to visit.) In fact you'll spot your first 'bergs before you even reach Antarctica, on your ship's rollercoaster crossing of the Drake Passage, south of Cape Horn. Captains are wary of getting too close to the ice, but with a pair of binoculars you can often spot groups of penguins (there are six species down here) going about their business — blissfully unaware that their colony has detached itself from the mainland and is drifting towards warmer climes.

Editor's tip: If you want penguins but could do without the ice, there's always South Africa. You can visit Simonstown, south of Cape Town — home to 3,000 African penguins — for perhaps a quarter of the £4,000-odd price of an Antarctic expedition.

Brighton Pier, East Sussex, UK

As this century-old relic rests its weary legs in the swell, day draws to an end and gulls circle overhead. But while dusk signals bedtime to the birds, things are just getting going on Brighton Pier. Peppered with 67,000 light bulbs, it illuminates the East Sussex shoreline either side. What's more, the old girl's still pulling in four million visitors a year (she's had almost 120 years of experience, after all), with the promise of ducks to hook, candyfloss to gorge on, fortunes to be made (albeit in 2p pieces) and 525m of walkway to amble along. Do it properly and immerse yourself in the unapologetically kitsch kiosks and fairground (complete with Isle of Wight views from the top of the helter-skelter).

Editor's tip: Parking in the town is tricky — and costly — so use the Park & Ride. Buses to the seafront run about every 15 minutes.

Praia da Concha, Portugal

Time for a roadtrip — south from the medieval seaside city of Porto to this dramatic stretch. A profusion of lesser-visited attractions make the two-hour drive worth stretching over a weekend. First stop: the lively, canal-laced town of Aveiro, gateway to the sweeping sand dunes and empty waterside trails of the Natural Reserve of São Jacinto. Then it's on to the sleepy fishing village, Palheiros da Tocha, before a glimpse of holidays Portuguese-style at the buzzy resort backing Figueira da Foz's great white sweep. Finally, abandon the car in São Pedro de Moel for a walk along one of the wooden paths from the cliffs towards this beach's pounding surf.

Editor's tip: *Pousadas* (historic hotel conversions) offer some of the best accommodation en route — from modern glass cubes, to medieval houses (pousadasofportugal.com).

Bazaruto Archipelago, Mozambique

The Maldives? Meh. You'll actually find the world's dreamiest *least-known* beaches just off the coast of Mozambique, on the five vanilla-white dollops of the Bazaruto Archipelago. Here, swathes of silky sand segue into seas of blue, while inland, dunes undulate like oversized Zen gardens. There are dolphins, turtles and whale sharks, but no soppy honeymooners or sightseers wielding selfie sticks — just you and the deep blue. True, Mozambique's civil war of 1977-1992 brought devastation to the East African republic, and the scars can still be seen in parts of the country, but the Bazaruto Archipelago was one of the first areas to recover — and the peace is now profound.

Editor's tip: Snorkel out to Two Mile Reef to swim with kingfish, turtles, honeycomb rays and, if you're very lucky, whale sharks.

Mount Fuji, Japan

For centuries, its peak was considered too sacred to be climbed (only monks scaled it until the 8th century AD; only men for the next 1,200 years). But today anyone can have a go during July and August — though the trails are steep and scrappy. There is another option: head to leafy Shizuoka province at the dormant volcano's southern flank. Here, in Japan's most prolific tea-growing area, you get picture-perfect views of the snow-topped summit *and* a perfect cuppa or two from the many plantations spread out in its shadows, watered by streams filled with melted mountain snow.

Editor's tip: If you do choose to hike, and are prone to altitude sickness (or aren't sure), spend a night at one of the basic communal huts at the midway point to acclimatise. Then wake two hours before dawn to complete the hike and see sunrise from the top.

Baja California, Mexico

There's the famous California, forever high on the holiday hit list. And there's the other one, which fewer know of: Baja California is a different kettle of fish. For starters it's in Mexico — grab a map and find it dangling off the west coast like a useless arm, Pacific Ocean one side, Sea of Cortez the other. If mass tourism has yet to fall for it, that's to the benefit of travellers with particular passions: surfing, sailing and deep-sea fishing. The oceanic waters are a bouillabaisse of life, notably here at Bahía Magdalena, where lagoons and barrier islands harbour turtles (including green and loggerhead) as well as blue and grey whales, down from the Arctic to calve. Sardine shoals swirl in balls, pursued by swordfish which, contrary to belief, don't spear their prey, but slash it terminally — or even shovel it out of the sea bed.

Editor's tip: Bahía Magdalena is an excellent spot for whale-watching because the small 'panga' boats that are commonly used can get up very close to the creatures.

160

Istanbul, Turkey

This is Hagia Sophia, just one of Istanbul's many swoon-worthy, yet cheap, attractions. Even the (free) walk here is a visual feast: at sunset, walk across Galata Bridge, which spans the gleaming waters of the Golden Horn. You'll pass dozens of anglers, their rods flexing promisingly as squawking seagulls cast their fleeting shadows from above. The smells of apple-infused tobacco drift up from cafes on the bridge's lower promenade, as the broad domes and slender minarets of the mosque stretch into an implausible sky. It's tempting to describe the sunset as saffron, but the expensive mounds of spice in the bazaar (five minutes from the end of the bridge; free) look rustier than this — pumpkin or honey would be more accurate.

Editor's tip: As you leave the bridge, stop at one of the bobbing boats tied to the quay and shell out for a giant grilled fish sandwich. As fine, filling meals go, it's another bargain at £3.

The Abacos, Bahamas

The soft sashay of palm tops, the sigh of a clear blue tide, the listless drift of sand along miles of white beach... The Bahamas seem to exist in a kind of syrupy half-sleep — especially the Abaco Islands, where Hope Town's pastel-pink houses appear to have been moulded from sugar paste, and even the jolly red-and-white-striped lighthouse looks like an oversized candy cane. Each July, the Junkanoo Summer Festival rolls into the region like a crepe-paper cyclone to shake the Bahamas from deep slumber. A riot of music, dance and costumes that gives Rio a run for its money, it makes landfall in Nassau and runs for the month.

Editor's tip: Some of the smaller islands, such as Great Abaco, host a more homely interpretation of the festival a month earlier (June). Queues for the zingingly spicy conch ceviche are considerably shorter...

Yellowstone National Park, USA

Like a portal to another dimension that opens only briefly, the largest hot spring in the USA blazes special-effects bright in September, then cools to a deep pine-green by winter. Thank the mineral-fuelled microbes at the water's edge for the extra-terrestrial orange that complements the copper colour of the escaping rivulets. And blame the Yellowstone Caldera (that's the world's largest 'supervolcano', naturally) for keeping the sapphire depths at the centre a simmeringly unswimmable 87°C. Instead of a dip, you'll do your marvelling from a boardwalk that snakes between Excelsior Crater and the Turquoise Pool in Wyoming's Midway Geyser Basin.

Editor's tip: Head to the northeast corner of the park, where the Yellowstone River winds through willow-wooded valleys, for the most spectacular colour shift.

The Himalayas

Meaning 'Abode of Snow' in Sanskrit, The Himalayas are the world's mightiest mountain range, running 2,400km across the rooftop of Asia, from Afghanistan to Bhutan. Unless you're Michael Palin, that is way too much mountain for one trip, but luckily it's *all* breathtakingly beautiful: from the mighty summits of Nepal and the timewarp traditional villages of Bhutan, to the Tibetan plateau and the temple towns of northern India, you can't go wrong. In India, Ladakh (aka Little Tibet) is a monastery-littered moonscape of high-plains deserts and peaks, reached via a 5,000m+ road only open in summer.

Editor's tip: Make like a *memsahib* and take the tiny 'Toy Train' to Darjeeling, where you can drink tea on the terrace at the Windamere Hotel and gaze across a sea of tea toward mighty Mount Kangchenjunga, Earth's third highest peak.

Longsheng, China

From a distance they appear machine-honed, so perfectly contoured are the rice terraces that throw their endless lassos around the hilly slopes of Longsheng County, in southern China. Which makes it surprising to learn that these stepped paddy fields have been a feature of local life since the Yuan Dynasty ruled in the 13th century. Given the paucity of ploughable land here in Guilin province (most famous for its otherworldly karst mountains), ingenuity was needed to ensure maximum irrigation and crop yield — but the Zhuang and Yao people, who have inhabited the region since ancient times, certainly had that. Now, as much as 1,100m above sea level in places, Longsheng (it means 'dragon's backbone', named for its overlapping-scale look) is heaven for hikers — not to mention photographers, after that prize-winning mist shot.

Editor's tip: While the terraces are beautiful as the seasons change, avoid visiting in autumn when they are at their least visually appealing: dry and stubbly after the harvest.

Marrakech, Morocco

It's easy to get lost in the twisting, orange-daubed alleys of the *medina* — but it's there, the old walled city, that you'll find Marrakech's finest tagine pots, Berber carpets, leather bags and strongly-scented spices. Because that's where the *souks* are —humming with transaction (seek the carpenters and blacksmiths on the market fringes for a glimpse of local retail). Start in the chaos of main square, Jemma el Fna, where snake-charmers jostle with henna tattooists, jewellery-sellers, food stalls and the odd motorbike. Next, wander at whim, stopping to haggle over souvenirs (these spice stalls near the grocers' *souk* look and smell incredible — but buying as a tourist can be more expensive than back at home, and quality varies considerably, so stop only for a photo). Then wind down with a fresh mint tea in a sidestreet cafe.

Editor's tip: When it comes to haggling, don't start the process unless you're serious about buying. Kick off with a bid that's around half the asking price — don't be put off by the feigned outrage — and go from there.

Fly Geyser, Nevada, USA

Some sights are *worth* trespassing for. But while these striking, multi-coloured mineral formations currently sit on private land, the good news is that it's about to open up to the public. Bought in 2016 by the Burning Man Project (the folks behind neighbouring Black Rock Desert's notorious annual festival of primal art, culture, torching giant effigies and 'radical self-expression' (i.e. nudity)), Fly Ranch is home to this surprisingly man-made geyser. (It was rumoured to have been created when scientists looking to harness the area's geothermal power drilled a test well at the site, then abandoned it, leaving the limey deposits that have created these curious mounds, belching boiling water.) It's noisy, it's smelly, it's disruptive — much like the festival itself.

Editor's tip: Sign up to the Fly Ranch volunteers' newsletter — you'll find it at flyranch.burningman.org/participate — and you'll know the minute the site is open to visitors.

Venice, Italy

You've ticked off the Piazza San Marco, Santa Croce, and the Grand Canal. Now get under the skin of this hard-to-fathom city. Head north from the tourist-heavy centre and you'll reach Cannaregio, where the real Venetians live. Here, no-nonsense cafes bordering the Ormesini Canal vend cheap espressos from the crack of dawn, while the medieval tenements of the old Jewish ghetto hide art galleries and antique shops. Or make for the easterly part of the Castello district for pastel-painted fishermens' houses strung with washing. Stroll here in the morning, via the bustling Via Garibaldi, and you'll wander past canal boats turned into market stalls, heaving with fresh fruit and veg.

 **Editor's tip:** Venetian restaurants are notoriously touristy and underwhelming, but the old Jewish ghetto has some of the city's best eateries. Try Gam Gam and its sister cafe, Gam Gam Goodies.

Plitvice Lakes National Park, Croatia

If you're already reaching for your swimming costume and inflatable ring, just hold on a second — the water here's not quite as warm as it looks. In fact we're deep in the forested heart of Croatia, towards the Bosnian border. And that totally tropical colour? It's to do with the play of light on the bed of chalk: as the current softly erodes the lake floor, it deposits the sediment in banks, which become fertile havens for mosses, seeds and offshoots drifting downstream. The result is a magical mix of elfish waterpark, CGI sci-fi scene, and a slightly crowded Garden of Eden — and it's been dazzling tourists for centuries.

Editor's tip: The main lakes tumble down the hillside, so take the panoramic train to the upper lakes then follow the cascades down on foot.

Ranthambore National Park, India

More than 70 per cent of the world's tigers live in India, and the population is rising. But that doesn't mean sightings are guaranteed — there are still only 2,300 in this vast country. Three hours' drive from Jaipur, in royal Rajasthan, the sprawling old hunting grounds of Ranthambore make a good place to try to find one (Prince Phillip did, in 1961, but then he shot it. Different times...). Set out as the sun rises over this epic jungle jumble, strewn with the ruins of ancient temples, and you might spot one of the 48 tigers that prowl its dense undergrowth. And if not, there are also wild boar, leopards and sloth bears...

Editor's tip: Luxury tents offer the park's best accommodation, designed to give a taste of the historic hunting camps. Pair this with a stay in a converted Rajasthani palace and live like a maharajah (tourism.rajasthan.gov.in).

Luskentyre Sands, Isle of Harris, UK

Transparent seas, soft white sands, cerulean skies... You say the Caribbean, we say Scotland. That's right, this Outer Hebridean beauty lies just 60km off the end of the A835 from Inverness. There's more to this sandbar than sand, of course — but, blessedly, not that much more. Huge dunes line the northern end; the odd settlement hunkers down among the wildflowers; and beyond that, there's only a huge sky and glorious emptiness. Some of the few visitors who make it this far west kitesurf, but most simply gaze towards the island of Taransay and scan the horizon for dolphins. Either way, save for the passing flash of a white pony, you're guaranteed solitude.

Editor's tip: One of the few buildings abutting the beach is Luskentyre Harris Tweed, supplier to several Savile Row tailors (and Nike!). Go and pick up some cut-price cloth.

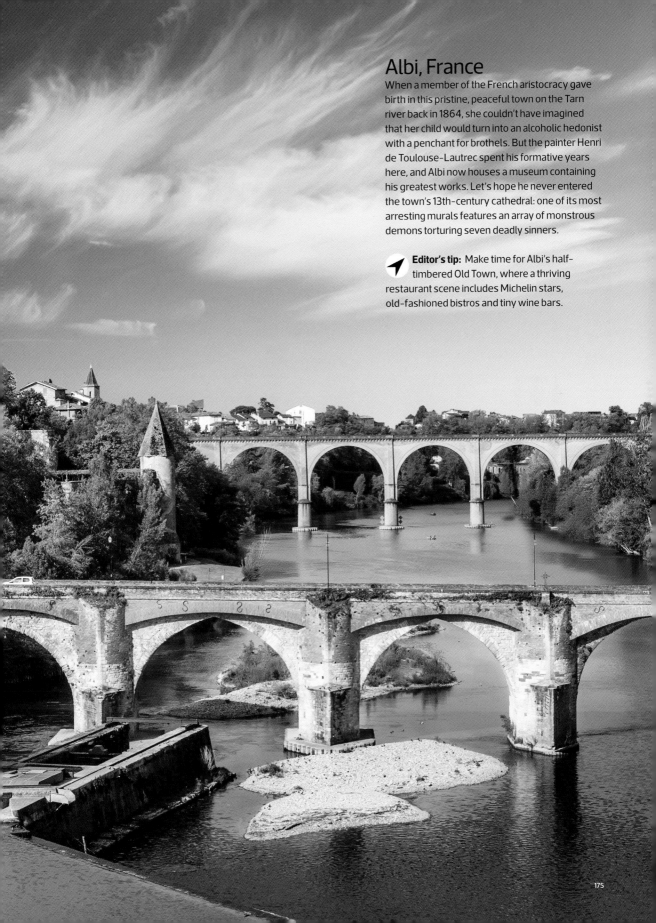

Albi, France

When a member of the French aristocracy gave birth in this pristine, peaceful town on the Tarn river back in 1864, she couldn't have imagined that her child would turn into an alcoholic hedonist with a penchant for brothels. But the painter Henri de Toulouse-Lautrec spent his formative years here, and Albi now houses a museum containing his greatest works. Let's hope he never entered the town's 13th-century cathedral: one of its most arresting murals features an array of monstrous demons torturing seven deadly sinners.

Editor's tip: Make time for Albi's half-timbered Old Town, where a thriving restaurant scene includes Michelin stars, old-fashioned bistros and tiny wine bars.

101 Tower, Taipei, Taiwan

Unlike so many skyscrapers, this building could *not* be just anywhere. With its proud winged shoulders puffed out in full pagoda style (a design inspired by a bamboo stalk) ,Taipei's 101 Tower is pure Asia. And its pride is justified — it was the world's tallest tower until Dubai's Burj Khalifa knocked it off its perch in 2010. This city, though it echoes with the same Mandarin patter as Beijing, has a mellowness and ease that the Chinese mainland lacks: there's no tourist visa necessary and no internet firewall; it's infinitely cleaner and less polluted. Even the tower itself is green, with waste-free restaurants and energy-saving insulation. It's a fitting icon for one of Asia's most progressive countries — the first to ban dog meat, diners will be pleased to hear.

Editor's tip: A reasonable 1 hour 40 minute flight from Hong Kong (around £60 one way), Taipei is best tacked on to a city break there, or a multi-stop Asia tour.

Fiordland National Park, New Zealand

They say you must set your watch back 20 years when you land in New Zealand — but make that 2,000 years for parts of South Island. Flanked by a foreverness of mountain running almost its entire 800km length, this is a land of pristine, timeless grandeur, perfect for its role as Middle-Earth in the *Lord of the Rings* films. Fiordland National Park is the star-turn — the five-day 'tramp' into Milford Sound is a phenomenal trek, topped only by kayaking on the sound once you're there — but South Island doesn't have to be hard work: for every rugged Kaikoura whale-watching trip, there's a sunny Marlborough winery to sample...

Editor's tip: Adrenaline junkies can feed their need in Queenstown, the birthplace of bungee-jumping, and now the all-whooping, undisputed global capital of adventure sports.

Bruges, Belgium

This city ticks all the boxes for a weekend away (particularly the chocolate ones). It's got canals and cobbles, beer and basilicas — and, of course, a profusion of the sweet stuff. Spend Saturday morning exploring by boat, before hitting the chocolatiers on Katelijnestraat. Then clamber up the 366 steps of Bruges's belfry, for views right across town. (Evenings are for *frites* and beer, preferably at the city's oldest pub, Herberg Vlissinghe.) Start the next day with a trip to one of myriad bakeries for just-baked pastries — perhaps posh Patisserie Academie on Vlamingstraat. Finally, savour a long wander round the Groeningemuseum, choc-a-bloc with Renaissance masterpieces.

Editor's tip: Go in December, when the Christmas Market in the main square, Grote Markt, brings extra, snow-dusted sparkle to the city. There's an ice rink, mulled wine and twinkling tree.

Aarhus, Denmark

It's hard not to take a rose-tinted view of the world from the top of Aros, the art museum in Aarhus, Denmark's charming second city. Crowning the cubic modern gallery like a giant disco light is *Your Rainbow Panorama* by Danish-Icelandic artist Olafur Eliasson. Stroll its circular walkway and your 150m-long circuit takes you through the spectrum: look outwards and you'll see canals turned orange, turquoise docks, medieval spires rendered pinky-purple; look down at yourself and see your own clothes transformed by the suffusing light. After that arty encounter it's time for canalside beers and aimless old-town wandering: a masterpiece of an afternoon.

Editor's tip: Come to Aarhus in late August and early September to find the city in full festival flow: art and music events — many free — flood the streets, while a food festival takes the party to the seaside.

Easter Island, Chile

Mystery clings to this tiny, isolated speck in the Pacific Ocean like moss to rock. Despite a dozen theories, no one truly knows where its people came from, where they went, or what their enigmatic stone faces represent. It's a fact that the indigenous population dwindled from 15,000-odd to almost zero in just three or four generations (deforestation? civil war? cannibalism?), and certainly these ancient Moai statues are carved from volcanic tuff... But for the rest of it? Go, see, and make up your own mind. (Arrive at dawn or dusk, when the Moai are at their most impressive, their expressions changing with the shifting light.)

Editor's tip: Other than the Moai, there's not *that* much here, so aim for February and the Tapati Rapa Nui Festival, a mad two-week celebration of the island's culture, with two clans competing in a series of music, dance and (often bizarre) sporting contests.

London, England

Every day during summer (and on Mondays, Wednesdays, Fridays and Sundays for the rest of the year), battalions of people turn up to see some squaddies swap shifts — otherwise known as 'Changing the Guard' at Buckingham Palace. But there's plenty more to do at the regal residence: book tickets to the State Rooms and Royal Mews and you can peek at Her Maj's gilded carriages and Old Masters. After that, it's a stroll to the capital's triumvirate of posh parks: St James's and Green Park come with deckchairs shaded by whispering trees. But Hyde Park is the must-do, thanks to the Serpentine. The lake has a lido, making it one of the few in London open to swimmers, while the neighbouring Serpentine Galleries are in two brilliantly contrasting London buildings — one traditional, one space-age — and also free to all.

Editor's tip: If you can live without the trumpets, the Changing of the Queen's Life Guard, up the road at Horse Guards Parade, is arguably more spectacular (it's on horses!) — and certainly less crowded, which means better views.

Great Barrier Reef, Australia

From the air it doesn't look much: a petri dish dappled with exotic fungus, perhaps, or a submerged archipelago of seaweed. With the Great Barrier Reef, however, the delight is in the detail. Strap on a mask and snorkel, and take the plunge into a world of alien beauty, where every square inch reveals an intricate microcosm of life. Anemones as outlandish as Muppets' haircuts waft in the currents, their neon tendrils providing shelter for white-ribboned clownfish. Schools of electric-blue fish dance between outcrops of coral in perfect synchronism, while hard-beaked parrotfish scatter layer upon ivory layer of sand on the seafloor — the by-product of their rocky diet. There are bigger fish here too: black-tip reef sharks patrol like sleek, silent sentinels... then disappear, ghost-like, back into the blue.

Editor's tip: Cairns is a popular base for reef visitors, but it can feel rather touristy. Instead, consider staying in chic Port Douglas, for its cool cafes and dreamy Four Mile Beach.

Mount Bromo, Java

It's a dream of a view — the first chink of sunrise revealing the black desert plains around this magnificent volcano swathed in a starlit mist — but Mount Bromo has a nightmarish side, too. It's one of 127 active volcanoes in Indonesia, last erupting as recently as July 2016, and sending a coil of smoke high into the sky. The event prompted a government ban on tourists entering a two-kilometre-wide exclusion zone, but still they come. And who can blame them? Beyond this remarkable scene, in the wild national park that surrounds the crater, there are glittering waterfalls, blankets of wild orchids, and glimpses of rare black leopards.

Editor's tip: Hundreds of tourists make the torchlit 3am trek up neighbouring Mount Penanjakan, the best viewpoint for Bromo's sunrise. Most finish at Viewpoint One, so it's worth climbing higher to Viewpoint Two, where the outlook is both more tranquil and more spectacular.

Chichén Itzá, Mexico

This stone giant, rising from dense jungle, dwarfs anyone who stands in its shadow — of all the temples at the mighty 8th-century Mayan site of Chichén Itzá, it's El Castillo that's the daddy. Architectural intimidation was the name of the game for the builders who created one of the most sacred spots in ancient Mexico: blood-chilling engravings of animals sneered from hidden corners; the high-sided ballcourt instilled terror in players (losers would be sacrificed); and petroglyphs depicting the Mayans' conquered victims wailed silent screams. You can still see the evidence — but you can escape it too: beyond is the Yucatán Peninsula, a tranquil paradise of lush jungle and Caribbean beaches.

Editor's tip: Most visitors bus in to Chichén Itzá and straight back out — but combine your trip with a stop in Valladolid town, a colourful contrast to high-rise Cancún.

Havasu Falls, Arizona, USA

Surreal, isn't it? So blue it could be a theme-park attraction. And yet it's all natural, simply the most spectacular cascade of a series created by Havasu Creek as it tumbles through a rust-red landscape to join the Colorado river just south of the Grand Canyon. The colour is created by limestone particles from subterranean caves which, dissolved, reflect blue daylight powerfully back — hence this pool, the hue of a cowboy's jeans. It's more than just a beauty spot, mind: the creek is a life-bringer for the Havasupai, whose nearby village, Supai, is cut off from the world in this dry, dusty desert canyon.

Editor's tip: The Falls are a 12km hike from the car park at Hualapai Hilltop, and the path isn't signposted, so it's hard to spot. The most reliable marker is the trail of mule dung — locals use the animals to get up to the Hilltop and back.

Sicily, Italy

Cut adrift in the middle of the Mediterranean, Sicily was a prized stepping stone on ancient European trade routes — Greeks, Romans, Phoenicians and Arabs have all left their mark. Their legacy? An endlessly interesting island with its own unique dialect and cuisine, artistic traditions and architecture, finding form in the crumbling chaos of Palermo and the Baroque hill towns of the south. Lying on roughly the same latitude as Tunis and Algiers, Sicily also enjoys proper, limb-loosening heat, with bone-white beaches for summer, and hillwalks on donkey tracks for spring and autumn.

Editor's tip: Sicily's southern corner is best, with long, sandy beaches and stunning towns in its hills, including Ragusa (setting for much of the *Inspector Montalbano* series), where a statue of St George is paraded through the labyrinth of lanes at Easter (pictured).

185

Taj Mahal, India

Few places are more astonishing in reality than they appear in photos. The Taj Mahal is one. As you pass through the gates, the first thing to strike you is the building's monumental size — skyscraper-high, its domes glistening pearl-like in the hazy light. Then as you approach, along the fountain-filled gardens, you begin to see the detail: tens of thousands of precious stones inlaid into the facade in finely traced floral filigree and sumptuous swirls. Finally, you enter the building itself, where the twin coffins of the emperor and his beloved wife, Mumtaz, sit serene, covered in exquisite kufic calligraphy behind lace screens carved, implausibly, from stone.

Editor's tip: Few know that you can see the Taj by moonlight, with just 50 other people, on the two nights either side of each month's full moon (tajmahal.gov.in). Stay in Agra town itself, where the Taj Mahal lies, and wake early: tickets are available from 8am at the East and West gates, hours before the coach parties arrive.

Dead Sea, Middle East

If you want to swim with fish, you're in the wrong place. Our scaly friends can't survive in the super-salty waters here, hence the somewhat gloomy name. Yet for humans, the Dead Sea, surrounded by Jordan, Israel and the West Bank, is utterly life-enhancing: a soak in the buoyant, mineral-thick solution is said to benefit people with skin, muscle, joint and heart complaints. And those with lung problems can breathe easy, too — the atmosphere is exceptionally oxygen-rich (its shores are the lowest on Earth, producing the opposite effect of being on a mountain peak). Marine life might not be able to survive in this sea, but you'll thrive in it.

Editor's tip: Both the Israeli and Jordanian banks are lined with big hotels, but there's no need for more than a day-trip here (and you can use their beaches and facilities for around £30). One more thing: the water stings. Don't shave any part of your body the day you visit...

Kirkjufell, Iceland

Its name translates as 'church mountain', and this ancient natural masterwork certainly resembles a huge cathedral, its spire watching over the Atlantic from Iceland's west coast. On the winter nights when the Northern Lights' otherworldly shadows dance across the sky and turn the neighbouring waterfall to gemstone, the view is more ethereal still. Yet most visitors only make a day trip to Kirkjufell from Reykjavík (two and a half hours' drive away), missing the mountain at its most spectacular; this means they also miss the lesser-visited waterfalls, lava fields and glaciers that surround it on the striking Snæfellsnes Peninsula.

Editor's tip: The Northern Lights aren't guaranteed in Iceland — and bear in mind that they don't show up this colourful to the naked eye. But for the best chance of seeing them, visit the north or west of the country, September to January, and allow at least a week to chase them.

Etosha National Park, Namibia

This is the safari with one important animal missing — the human. While 1.7 million tourists pack South Africa's Kruger park every year, people are lesser-spotted in its Namibian equivalent, Etosha, which gets only 200,000 visitors annually. It's not for want of wildlife — four of the Big Five live here (buffalo can't stand the high temperatures), alongside dancing impala, prowling cheetah and these graceful zebra, who create zigzagging patterns of dizzifying proportions as they mass around Etosha's busy watering holes. Beyond the safari camps, Namibia has much more to offer: combine a stay in Etosha with time on its dramatic, shipwreck-strewn Skeleton Coast, or the sun-scorched mountains of the Damaraland desert.

Editor's tip: Go in October, when the dry heat means animals stay near the watering holes and are therefore easy to spot — you can see up to 300 at a time.

Lake Waikopiro, New Zealand

Almost looks like Britain, doesn't it? But you couldn't be further from home: New Zealand's Lake Waikopiro is an ancient hunting ground for the Maori of North Island. Along with its larger neighbour, Lake Tutira, this freshwater stretch creates a rare and stunning national conservation area. If you're angling for a little action, there are huge rainbow trout lurking beneath the surface; or look up and spot feathered fantails, Australian swamp-hens and little shags you certainly wouldn't see in the wintry skies over Britain.

Editor's tip: Twin with the nearby city of Napier, New Zealand's Art Deco beauty. Its Art Deco Festival (February) is a 1930s-themed blow-out of fancy-dress, Prohibition-style parties and vintage cars (artdeconapier.com). Or try the weekly Urban Food Market on Saturday for coffee, pies and puddings.

Empty Quarter, Oman

It's rare to find a place that's got less busy over the centuries, but this vast, 650,000sq km desert once featured on the well-trodden trade route to Sumhuram, where frankincense was bought and sold. More than 2,000 years ago, the resin harvested from the local trees was more precious than gold, and merchants came all the way from Israel to obtain it, through modern-day Jordan, Saudi Arabia and Yemen, on a journey that took around 200 days. Follow Oman's UNESCO-listed section of the trail, and you'll drive empty desert highways towards the ruins of three cities, including the oasis of Shisr where the ancient camel caravans would stop to rest, the majority of it now buried by sand.

Editor's tip: Roads are long and isolated, and accidents (often involving stray camels) are frequent. Opt for a driver rather than a hire car.

Paro Taktsang, Bhutan

Clinging to a rockface in the lush Upper Paro Valley, the jumble of white and gold that is Paro Taktsang — or Tiger's Nest — seems to have sprouted straight from the stone. The closer you trek, the more the precipitous construction baffles, especially when you learn that Bhutan's most sacred temple complex — centered around the cave of Buddhist founding father Guru Padmasambhava — was built in this remote spot in 1692. How did they do it? You'll have plenty of time to ponder the question as you approach the turreted buildings and rainbow-hued prayer flags flapping in the breeze; Paro Taktsang is only accessible by foot, and visitors must complete a five-hour round-trip hike to reach its doors. But if there's such a thing as the stairway to heaven, this is it.

Editor's tip: Pack light: bags, phones and cameras aren't allowed inside the monastery.

Manhattan, New York

Blessed with a city of straightforward grid lines and manageable distances, New Yorkers are walkers, by and large— and sauntering should be obligatory for visitors since it delivers instant sensory immersion in the most electric city on the planet. Yet for footsore club-goers, jetlagged sightseers, and frozen mid-winter shoppers, nothing warms the soul quite like the sight of an NYC taxi, approaching in a blur of yolk-yellow (paint shade Dupont M6284, to be exact; the officially prescribed colour since the 1960s). They're easily flaggable (raise your arm, making sure first that the white roof light is on), cheap, and licensed for four passengers. In central Manhattan, don't bother trying to hail the more recently introduced lime-green variety — these cabs can only pick up in outer boroughs and northern Manhattan neighbourhoods. Or, of course, you could always walk...

Editor's tip: Don't give your destination as an address — you need to be armed with the intersection details (eg, 'Lexington and 57th') — and don't even bother trying to get a cab between 4 and 5pm: that's when drivers change shift, so half of them are headed home.

Plaza de España, Seville

No one does a city square quite like the Spanish.
Take Seville's Plaza de España — a showpiece
1920s pleasure park and underrated sight hidden
in the lush, almost tropical Parque de María Luisa.
Built in 1928 for a big-stakes Spanish-American
expo, its regal painted staircases, fizzing fountains
and horseshoe moat all demand a good camera —
and an obliging model. But where to pose first on
this broad, flat stage? Do as the locals do, and head
for the densely tiled, blue, green and gold Provincial
Alcoves — it's not uncommon for Spanish tourists
to come and snap a selfie beside their home region's
alcove, so don't feel silly as you drape over the
austere royal murals and mosaic maps. So much of
Seville's flavour comes after dark (late nights, poky
bars and slim, canopied alleyways), that this broad,
bright plaza is a huge, welcome lungful of fresh air.

Editor's tip: Plaza de España opens early
compared with Seville's other sights (9am).
Most locals won't even be out of the door then —
so go first thing for the perfect panorama.

Quintana Roo, Mexico

Scattered along the postcard-perfect coastline of the Mayan Riviera, thousands of underwater caves make a dramatic change from all that sun and sand. The bravest visitors freedive them, heading up to 20m down into the big blue with nothing more than a snorkel and mask, to swim between great stalactites and ribbons of neon fish. But the cenotes are also open to less intrepid swimmers and snorkellers, who come to bask in the green glow of their limestone-filtered fresh-water, or watch turtle and goldfish darting just below the surface.

Editor's tip: For leisurely day trips, Cenote Azul near Playa del Carmen is one of our favourites. Freedivers prefer Dos Ojos or El Pit, both near Tulum.

Mosel River, Germany

This green dollop might appear to be an island, but it's an optical illusion — caused by the Mosel River turning a great loop right by the wine-making town of Bremm. Here, some of the vine-blanketed terraces that trim the water are so steep that grapes have to be harvested the old-fashioned way: by hand. Visitors can traverse the vineyards too, on rugged hiking trails that zigzag through the crops. The reward? Top-notch Riesling with change from 10 euros. Less energetic enthusiasts might prefer to take a hire car: Bremm is a stop on Germany's 243km Mosel Wine Route, which zooms past fairytale castles, Roman ruins and imposing abbeys on its way from Perl on the French border to photo-op city of Koblenz.

Editor's tip: Up the holiday ante with a Mosel river cruise, past half-timbered houses and medieval villages. A handful of companies offer week-long trips, with boats ranging from basic to all-out five-star grandeur.

Boudhanath Stupa, Kathmandu, Nepal

Cradled between India and Tibet, Nepal is a mystical mish-mash of cultural influences. Formerly the world's only Hindu Kingdom (until royal rule ended in 2007), Nepal nevertheless has Buddhist blood coursing through its veins. Dominating the Kathmandu Valley skyline for around 1,500 years, Boudhanath Stupa (the burial monument pictured) is its most famous face, but wherever you go you'll find Buddhist temples, shrines, and prayer flags fluttering from rooftops and summits. Trekking is Nepal's USP, with eight of the world's 10 highest mountains, and (literally) breathtaking hikes to the foot of Everest and Annapurna via lush forests and dramatic, glacial wilds. The Annapurna Circuit is probably one of the best long-distance treks in the world and makes many travellers' bucket lists. If it's on yours, allow up to 25 days for a trip, in order to acclimatise.

Editor's tip: Often overlooked but a brilliant two- or three-day add-on to any Nepal itinerary, Chitwan is a superb, pocket-sized national park, teeming with birdlife, tigers and rhinos.

Sydney Harbour Bridge

This view across the harbour from Milsons Point is pretty magical, but is reduced to runner-up status by the hair-tousling panorama from the *top* of the Sydney Harbour Bridge, a hulking steel bicep that moonlights as a giant climbing frame for anyone brave enough to take it on. Towering at 134m above the harbour's kingfisher-blue waters, it's the tallest bridge of its type in the world — twice as high as the sculptural, scallop-shell-white Opera House lying in its shadow. The knee-trembling, 1,332-step ascent takes you from the moss-dripping underbelly, along the inside arch and above the roaring traffic, before becoming a ladder for the final push to the summit.

Editor's tip: If you require a gulp of Dutch courage beforehand, head for the Harbour View Hotel, whose top-floor bar's balcony looks out over the bridge's lower rungs — along which you'll soon be teetering. Book your climb through Bridge Climb Sydney (bridgeclimb.com).

Ditchling Beacon, South Downs, UK

Feeling artistic stirrings? You're in good company. This bit of Sussex has provided inspiration for creative types from sculptor Eric Gill, via the writers and artists of the Bloomsbury Group, to *Snowman* creator Raymond Briggs. Orchids sway in the breeze while butterflies, lapwings and curlews swirl overhead. The area's also a magnet for ramblers and mountain-bikers (in fact the name 'Beacon' comes from the fact this chalk hill was the only spot high enough to warn of imminent invasion). Arrive early and head off, on foot or bike, along its bramble-lined bridleways. The ground may not rise above 248m, but on a clear day, with the landscapes rolling into infinity, you might just feel like you're walking in the air.

Editor's tip: The bridleway to Ditchling Beacon starts at the National Trust car park off Ditchling Road.

Kandy, Sri Lanka

It's so quiet, you can hear the fish swim. But only at dawn, as the sun rises above the mountains and lazily licks up the mist hovering on the water's surface. Sinhalese slaves dug this phallic waterhole two centuries ago to serve the royal palace and the Temple of the Sacred Tooth. Over time, natural brooks flowed down from the hills sweeping in tilapia and carp — and, as fishing was always forbidden, monitor lizards slunk in like alligators to take up the job. Watch a head bob up then disappear in a ripple as an egret swoops too late. By the time you complete the 3km loop, the tuk-tuks will have begun to swarm like wasps, the vendors will have set up their displays of Fanta, and the fish will have regained their privacy. Until tomorrow.

Editor's tip: Escape the heat at Pub Royale, the dim, tranquil throwback bar of the 160-year-old Queen's Hotel, which overlooks the lake.

Abraham Lake, Alberta, Canada

Tim Burton couldn't make it up: pockets of methane gas burped out by bacteria as they munch on the remains of decaying organisms on the lake bottom. As the bubbles rise to the water's surface — tinted milky-blue by minerals washed in during spring's glacier melt — they're trapped by the icy layer, then frozen in suspended animation like an army of jellyfish rising from the depths. And because Abraham serves as a reservoir, the water levels are constantly fluctuating, creating fantastical cross-hatch patterns in its depths. But don't be fooled by its alien beauty: the ever-shifting surface leads to thin ice, and if you were to expose one of those air pockets to an open flame, it would blow like TNT — a cinematic climax you don't want to risk.

Editor's tip: Go in December, when the bubbles are freshly frozen — by March they'll be gone.

Morris Island Lighthouse, South Carolina, USA

Imagine you're a trader from Georgian England, travelling to America to bundle your crop of indigo. The sentry in this picture would have been your first glimpse of the New World, as your boat wove amid the grassy marsh to the harbour at Charleston. Well more or less, anyway. This is the third lighthouse on the jetty, and we're lucky it's survived: water traffic has eased since Union fighters torched Charleston and industry died off, and a brutal earthquake knocked the structure askew, too, creating a nautical Tower of Pisa. The earth around it has also eroded, as you'll see if you make it to Lighthouse Inlet on Folly Island, so the drive takes you across wetlands into an outback of cottages on stilts, until the road ends altogether. Now walk the remaining pebbles to the chalky beach while windswept reeds hiss — and *breathe*.

Editor's tip: The current is too strong for swimming, but you can take sunset boat tours with sightings of bottlenose dolphin practically guaranteed (tidelinetours.com).

Colosseum, Rome

The squeamish should *not* dig deep into the history of the Colosseum. Inaugurated in 80AD, in its gladiatorial g(l)ory years the amphitheatre hosted some 50,000 spectators. The Emperor and his senators got the front row, cheering and jeering as gladiators fought, and lions, tigers and bears sprang from hatches in the floor to savage defenceless Christians. After Rome's 5th-century decline, the building fell into disrepair, overrun with exotic vegetation that sprouted from seeds carried in the dung of imported beasts. Today it's still the original horror of the place that permeates as you explore — ideally after dark, when it's eerily silent.

Editor's tip: With a guide, you'll access areas closed to the public: the sinister stage, covered with sand (as it once was, to soak up blood); and, down in the dungeons, the narrow tunnels where men waited in dread of their fate.

Geiranger Fjord, Norway

What do you see when you look at that waterfall? Because if it's 'Seven young sisters dancing playfully down the mountain', you've got what it takes to be a farmer in the Norwegian fjords. For when they weren't tending herds or turfing rooves, it seems, those guys were making up legends about waterfalls like it was going out of fashion (it's not just 'The Seven Sisters' here, but 'The Suitor', up the fjord, allegedly plying this lot with his splashy charms). Still, there wasn't much other entertainment: remote Geiranger Fjord freezes to the point of unreachability in winter. No wonder those farms are now so prettily abandoned...

Editor's tip: A 'Norwegian Fjords' cruise is the best way to see the area, but ship excursions are pricey. At Geiranger, as at any port of call, you can get identical — but much cheaper — trips just by googling 'cruise excursions'.

Canouan, St Vincent and the Grenadines

Lie back, let the masseur do their thing, and relax. But try hard not to nod off: the last thing you'll want to do in one of these over-water spa pavilions — a boat ride away from Canouan Resort — is miss *that* blue view. As the therapist attends to your knotted muscles, the sun reflecting off the sea's surface sends a palette of Caribbean blues into the room. Gaze out through the open side of the thatched palapa hut and you'll probably glimpse dolphins flickering across Carenage Bay. Now peer down through the face cradle in your massage table: the hut has a glass floor, through which you can watch eagle rays, sea turtles and nurse sharks as they make guest appearances among the resident fish, sponges and crustaceans on the reef below. Yes, this is paradise (albeit with paper pants on).

Editor's tip: The Grenadines might sound (and look) like the ends of the Earth, but Canouan is just a 35-minute flight from Brit-favourite Barbados; you can easily build a one-night trip into your holiday (canouan.com).

The Camargue, France

This is France, but not as you know it. Semi-feral horses thunder across the plains, wild bulls wallow in rice paddies, and flocks of flamingos wade across stark salt marshes: you'd never guess this rough-and-ready region, between the Med and the Rhône, was just an hour from the lavender fields of Provence. Beyond the wildlife and landscapes, the Camargue is a cultural curiosity, too — it's got more in common with earthy Spain, just across the Pyrenees, than with the rest of cosmopolitan France. Astride sturdy white horses, *gardians* (cowboys of the Camargue) spend their days rounding up cattle, the strongest of which appear in local bullfights. The venerable way of life informs everything from the food to the architecture, and the best way to experience it is on a ranch.

Editor's tip: While Spanish bullfights end in the animal's death, here they're usually a test of daring, and the bulls are fought, not stabbed.

River Li, China

A winged silhouette flits over the still river, a spectral refugee from a willow-pattern world that's fading fast; its master — balanced on his narrow bamboo raft, flickering lantern at the bow — is among the last cormorant fishermen of China. The birds dive for fish, then bob on the surface, throats bulging — the fishermen place a loop gently around the birds' necks to stop them swallowing all their catch. It's ingenious in its simplicity, yet this millennium-old way of life is on the decline: younger fishermen are lured away by more modern practices (and modern cities), leaving the old-timers up the creek — and one of China's oldest industries — without a paddle.

Editor's tip: The River Li runs from Guilin to Yangshuo (83km), in Guangxi Province; cruises are easy to book and take around six hours. Bear in mind dawn and dusk are the only times you'll catch these fishermen at work.

Faroe Islands

An English serviceman stationed here during the war rechristened the Faroe Islands 'The Land of Maybe' — maybe you'd see them, maybe you wouldn't; maybe you could land at the airport, maybe not. But the British military has itself to blame: our boys built the airstrip on Vágar Island to be invisible from the sea — but sometimes it's invisible from the air, too. It's certainly one of the more exciting approaches you'll make in the modern aviation world (this is where all Faroes' flights land). More or less equidistant from Iceland and Scotland, the islands have an Icelandic volcanic geology and a Scottish fondness for knitwear and sheep. They're now administered by Denmark and have a rugged, outpost beauty all of their own.

Editor's tip: Summer is as stable as the weather gets here — days are longer, and evenings are lighter (19.5 hours of daylight in June).

Frégate Island, Seychelles

Rarefied sightings come as standard on this exclusive island resort — but we don't mean the Beckhams, McCartneys or Jolie-Pitts, all of whom have holidayed here. No, the real stars of this natural paradise, 50km east of the capital, Victoria, are even more glamorous: white tropicbirds streak the skies; blue pigeons sing from fig trees; Seychelles magpie-robins, recently rescued from the brink of extinction, peer through the tropical canopy. At ground level, budding 'half-flower' plants provide sanctuary for nesting hawksbill turtles, while Aldabra giant tortoises graze on the dunes. Of course, there are other lovely (less expensive) beaches in the Seychelles, but it's more fun keeping up with the Zeta-Joneses. And the turtles.

Editor's tip: Frégate is a private island resort; expect to pay around £10,000 per week, including flights.

Barcelona, Spain

Littered with outré public art, Barcelona is a city of hedonistic excess. It helps explain why visitors imagine the architecture of its most famous son, Antoni Gaudí, to have sprung from a mind tinged with narcotics and/or insanity. (The sight of his unfinished basilica, the Sagrada Família, suggests as much, from the splayed columns of its Passion Façade to the tips of its garish pinnacles.) The reality is the opposite, though: a pious individual, Gaudí was umbilically linked to rural Catalonia, where he was born and raised. A fascination for vegetation and rough local construction materials remained with him as his career evolved; so did a passion for the identity of Medieval Catalonia — its tradesmen and mythology. And so Casa Milà, his psychedelically wavy apartment block, is also called La Pedrera ('The Quarry'). The druggy dragon-scaled roof of Casa Batlló is a reference to St George's nemesis. And the melty roofs of Park Güell's gatehouses are a nod to mushrooms — just not the magic kind.

Editor's tip: In the Gràcia district, seek out Gaudí's colour-soaked Casa Vicens. Few do.

215

Albuquerque, New Mexico, USA

Every October, there's a strange harvest in the suburban gardens of Albuquerque. 'Droppers' they call them: hot-air balloons that stray from the thermals above the New Mexican city, lose altitude and — *thwup* — land in locals' yards. Most reckon it's a small price to pay for the eccentric event that Albies have taken to their hearts. Launched in 1972, the Albuquerque International Balloon Fiesta is now the world's largest gathering of its type: a nine-day jamboree attracting 550 balloonists, 850,000 skyward gawpers, and craft shaped like cows and soda-pop cans. To many, the brutal beauty of central New Mexico is as much of a draw as the balletics above: the glowing-red Sandia Mountains, the metallic flash of the Rio Grande and those miles-upon-miles of deep-green cottonwood stands.

Editor's tip: Arrive at 7am on day one to see the Mass Ascension, when balloonists from around the world fill the skies to the strains of their national anthems.

Fushimi Inari Taisha, Kyoto, Japan

If Tokyo is Japan's tomorrow, Kyoto is its captivating past. The capital for more than 1,000 years, Kyoto was spared WWII bombs, so whispers of its ancient past still abound: a Buddhist temple here, a Shinto shrine there, narrow alleys and wooden houses in between. You can't see all 2,000 temples and shrines, but Fushimi Inari Taisha is a must. Pre-dating the capital's move to Kyoto in 794, the temple is famed for its vermilion *torii* gates (pictured), straddling a network of trails leading to sacred Mount Inari. It takes two hours, passing through 10,000-odd *torii* gates to reach the summit shrine on foot, but the city views from Yotsutsuji (about 30 minutes in) are reward enough for most.

Editor's tip: A one-week Japan Rail Pass costs only slightly more than a Tokyo-Kyoto return train fare, yet opens up the country to you. Invest in one.

Taverna, Greece

They might seem like 'Greek food 101', but *kalamarakia* — golden swirls of tender, deep-fried squid — are deceptively complex. You might notice they're listed twice on your menu: that'll be the fresh-off-the-boat stuff, and the frozen, breadcrumbed rings. Yes, Greek tavernas often keep a freezer stash, so politely check that what you're ordering is '*freska*'. The real deal has a loose, translucent batter, with whole mini-squid often jumbled up with the rings. It's a staple of this country's languid, breezy lunches, spent gazing over rocky bays or sun-dappled harbours.

Editor's tip: The other unofficial rules of taverna life? Dine late (2pm lunches, 9pm dinners); ask what's been caught that day; even better, visit the kitchen to see for yourself; share everything; and don't be sniffy about any toddlers or stray cats that pop up at your restaurant table.

Lake Pehoé,
Patagonia, Chile

They lour barrenly, but the foothills of those spiky peaks and surrounding scrubland in the Torres del Paine National Park are a breeding ground for pumas, foxes and the llama-like guanaco. People come too, to hike the trails around ancient forests, icy glaciers and languid lakes; the famous five-day W Trek is most popular. Or take the easy option and do a day trip: it's a three-hour bus ride to Pudeto from Puerto Natales, the nearest town; from there a catamaran scoots you across Lake Pehoé to Refugio Paine Grande — your bed for the night. However you get here, hard way or easy, the views will knock your socks off.

Editor's tip: Even during the Patagonian summer it's possible to witness four seasons in one day, so bring waterproofs and thermals as well as sunscreen and a hat.

Algar de Benagil, Portugal

A short boat trip from the Algarve coast, the Algar de Benagil is a cathedral cave — a grotto lit by light flooding in from a hole in the ceiling, known locally as 'the eye'. Understandably, it's a popular spot for photographers, who throng here to snap the sun's rays shining onto its hidden beach. Take a trip either from Benagil, where fishing boats bask on the sand beside a rainbow of sun umbrellas, or from the rugged ribbon of Praia da Marinha, where wave-smashed cliffs make sculptures in the sea. Along this stretch of coastline, there are hundreds of other caves ripe for exploration — some gloomy and partially submerged, others pummelled to nothing more than archways above the water.

Editor's tip: If you want the cave to yourself, eschew the tours in favour of an early morning kayak round the coast from Benagil.

Olhuveli Island, Maldives

Leave the sunsets to the starry-eyed honeymooners, because the best views in the Maldives are of the heavens, not the horizon. Olhuveli Island is just the spot for lazy astronomers. Home to the only hotel in the Laamu Atoll, it's 250km south of the resort-ringed capital Malé, so there's no light pollution to spoil the view — which, just north of the Equator, encompasses constellations from the northern and southern hemispheres. Lie back on Leaf Beach to savour the scene as a huge spring moon hangs low over the palm fronds. With your naked eye, you'll see the Milky Way shimmering across the sapphire sky, the occasional meteor blazing through it like a firework.

Editor's tip: That hotel on Olhuveli is the Six Senses Laamu, from £385 a night — but, like all Maldivian resorts, cheaper if booked with flights through a tour operator.

Prosecco Road, Treviso, Italy

How's this for a holiday with added sparkle? Italy has a Prosecco Road — and it's more than 30km long. Following the liquorice-lace country lanes an hour inland from Venice, it winds through vine-terraced hills between the towns of Conegliano and Valdobbiadene; stop off at tiny wineries where cheese and antipasti are served up with the tastings. Pootling on, stop to eat something more substantial at one of the region's ravishing hilltop restaurants, and clear fuzzy wine heads in the frescoed shade of San Salvatore castle (pictured) or the cool shadows of Follina's arched, 12th-century abbey.

Editor's tip: Choosing which of Prosecco Road's 30 wineries to visit can be hard, but make time for Garbara (widely agreed to make the region's best fizz), and Villa Sandi, housed in a magnificent Palladian villa.

Aït Benhaddou, Morocco

Behind these high mud walls sits a 300-year-old city, abandoned by all but four families. Rising from the terracotta foothills of the High Atlas Mountains, it was once a stop-off for camel trains travelling between Sudan and Morocco, but the delicate clay buildings and lack of electricity have caused a modern-day exodus. Aït Benhaddou isn't deserted, though: it gets plenty of visitors thanks to its UNESCO status and starring roles (in *Gladiator* and *Game of Thrones*). Now bright kaftan and carpet shops paint its perimeters, while the hum of hikers whispers through the shady alleys.

Editor's tip: Though many visit on day trips from Marrakech, it's a four-hour drive. Consider overnighting at one of the town's superb guesthouses, and you'll be rewarded with star-strewn, unpolluted night skies.

Grand Mosque, Abu Dhabi, UAE

By day, its white marble walls gleam like new porcelain, but come dusk the Grand Mosque takes on an unusual depth — as if its snowy surfaces are cloaking reds and blues beneath. See the four gold-tipped minarets glimmer in the last flashes of sun, then stay on as late as 8pm, watching the rows of archways glow majestically. You'll need this long to explore: the largest mosque in the UAE can hold 40,000 worshippers, and has countless treasures — including intricate floral designs inlaid with mother-of-pearl and lapis lazuli, 24-carat gold chandeliers, and the world's largest loomed carpet, hand-knitted by 1,200 craftsmen over two years.

Editor's tip: Check prayer times in advance, and be there just before — the haunting call to prayer, as it rings out over the marble walls, brings this magnificent building to life.

Walt Disney World, Florida, USA

'Epcot Center.' 'Geosphere.' 'The golf ball.' You're all wrong. The flagship attraction at Epcot, one of six theme parks that make up Walt Disney World Florida, is actually called Spaceship Earth. (Squirrel that one away for the next pub quiz. You're welcome.) Inside, visitors strap themselves into space-agey cars before taking a time trip: from prehistoric man, through the Renaissance, to modern day. It's History GCSE come to life. Which is pretty much what Epcot was all about when it was built in 1981: education + rollercoasters. If the kids are having fun, they won't even realise they're learning...

Editor's tip: Epcot's best feature isn't a ride, but the World Showcase — 11 countries recreated around a lake. It might sound gimmicky, but actually it's beautifully detailed, and there's nothing quite like taking a Venetian vaporetto from a British pub to a Japanese temple.

Salar de Uyuni , Bolivia

It's a long road. Or is it? It's hard to tell on Bolivia's Salar de Uyuni, where the salt crust is so flat and empty you lose all sense of size, distance and perspective. Spreading out like Arctic ice beneath a neon-blue sky, the 10sq km expanse makes up the world's largest salt pan. In the wet season, between January and April, water pools on the surface creating an enormous mirror, swallowing the horizon and making it impossible to tell where the Altiplano sky ends and the earth begins. But in the dry season, all moisture recedes, and the glaringly white surface cracks into geometrical patterns, like enormous dinosaur scales, and the salt crystals crunch under your sandals as you stroll out onto the moonscape surface.

Editor's tip: There's more to Bolivia than the Salar de Uyuni — a classic itinerary would include La Paz, Lake Titicaca, and Sun Island.

Blue Cypress Lake, Florida, USA

So that's not a cypress, and it's not blue. Fraud? No, the lake gets its name from the glow of trees at its perimeters, reflecting the water's surface in the strange dawn light. Even odder, Blue Cypress Lake is just an hour's drive from Disney World — though it couldn't feel further from the park's brash magic, and is well worth the detour. Book a boat trip here and you'll skim across silent water in search of nesting osprey, fishing herons and the occasional alligator, floating near the mangroves like a particularly dangerous log.

Editor's tip: Middleton's Fish Camp runs all tours and accommodation on the lake (middletonsfishcamp.com). Its cabins are basic and over-priced, but the more adventurous can camp lakeside for free, and there are showers.

Florence, Italy

No matter how many art books, postcards or
tacky kitchen aprons you've seen, nothing quite
prepares you for the moment you first gaze upon
the David. Rising a towering 5.17m in snowy
Carrara marble, Michelangelo's masterpiece —
in Florence's Accademia gallery — throbs with life,
muscles rippling and veins pulsating as he stares
defiantly towards his invisible enemy. Sculpted
from one lump of marble from 1501 to 1504, he
was originally destined to grace the roofline of
the russet Duomo, another Florence highlight —
but his godly good looks instead won him a spot
outside stately Palazzo Vecchio, the town hall.
Today, it's only a replica outside the Palazzo, but
he's still worth a snap... and you're a minute's walk
from one of Florence's finest coffee shops, Rivoire.

Editor's tip: Entry to the Accademia gallery
is timed; book your tickets well in advance
at b-ticket.com, choosing the very first morning
slot, and arrive early so you can head up the queue.

Great Wall, China

'Another name for the Great Wall,' you'll hear from your guide at some stage, 'is the Longest Cemetery in China. Most of the job was done by criminals — a kind of capital punishment.' The last word has resonance for the unfit day-tripper, stopping with traumatised lungs at the top of another switchback ascent. (The going is rock-face-rough in places.) At least you're never going to attempt the full length, though, which is... not known precisely, what with so many stretches gnawed away by time. Fortunately, this tract at Jinshanling (only two hours' drive from Beijing) is well preserved, a 10.5km dragon's back spiked with watchtowers. Built during the Ming Dynasty to repel the Mongols, it zigzags to the horizons: a spectacular view to sit and study, as your lungs recover.

Editor's tip: The cable car up is hot, small and cramped. Hike if you're claustrophobic. Want to walk further? September is the most temperate month — thus the best for trekking.

Logar Valley, Slovenia

Show this tree to a Slovenian and they'll gasp nostalgically as a Brit might upon catching a re-run of the old Yellow Pages 'J. R. Hartley' commercial. That's because pretty 'Logar's Linden' — protected as part of Slovenia's national heritage — has been the star of the country's most famous tourism TV ad since 1986 (almost literally the country's poster boy). Hardly surprising: near the Austrian border, it is one beautiful Alpine arbor, as devastating under a dusting of snow as it is in summer sunshine. In spring, you might follow the valley's nature trail (two-three hours), photograph waterfalls (Rinka Falls is the most awesome), or rent a mountain bike. As the advert says: 'Dobrodošli v Sloveniji!' — Welcome to Slovenia!

Editor's tip: Waterfalls are most powerful after winter's snow has melted, so spring is when to see them. Their strength dwindles by summer.

Halnaker, West Sussex, UK

It may seem like a scene from Enid Blyton's *The Enchanted Wood*, but this tree tunnel near the hamlet of Halnaker isn't make-believe. In fact, it's just 10 minutes from busy Chichester: the track follows a section of Stane Street — the laser-straight, flint-paved road that Roman conquerors built to link the city with London. Today the path is plied by ramblers and photographers, wandering beneath the intertwined branches of oak, hazel and black bryony. Crunch onwards and upwards to Halnaker Hill for panoramas of the undulating South Downs rolling away to infinity.

Editor's tip: If you're here in autumn to see these changing colours, make for nearby Slindon. Every October, this sleepy West Sussex village puts on spectacular tableaux of pumpkins, squashes and gourds in a festival that draws visitors from around the world.

Burano, Venice

It's pure visual Viagra, this little island, 40 minutes by *vaporetto* across the waters from Venice. Candy-coloured streets line canals tinted a vigorous mint-green, and even the bell tower juts into the sky at a jaunty angle. Those facades? Down through the centuries they've been gaily painted in jarring tones so that, the story goes, their fisher-folk residents could spot them through fog on the approach home. On a sunny day it's a treat to wander, past lace shops with their snowflake-like creations, stitched as they have been for centuries. Be sure to buy some before you leave — Burano is one of the few places in the world where the craft is still practised.

Editor's tip: Stay for lunch — it being a fishermen's island, you can count on stellar seafood; Jamie Oliver favours Trattoria al Gatto Nero, where fish risotto might be followed by baked turbot (gattonero.com).

Bora Bora, French Polynesia

Take that, Instagram. The ultimate holiday boast awaits, right on the other side of the world. It takes dedication to make the three-day, three-flight trip to this part of the South Pacific, but after two minutes with your feet in its flour-soft sand, you'll know it's been worth it. An extinct volcano, edged in coral-fringed lagoon and surrounded islets, Bora Bora is the stuff of castaway fantasies — which may explain its liberal scattering of five-star-plus resorts full of photogenic honeymooners. Join them and you'll understand why the island's first name was *Pora Pora Mai Te Pora*, which translates as 'created by the gods'.

Editor's tip Despite the posh resorts, you can stay cheaply — you'll get change from £80 per night at a basic guesthouse, booked through a consolidator site (try Booking.com).

Grand Canyon, USA

The trouble with the world's natural wonders is the people. They photobomb your sunset shot, interrupt quiet moments of contemplation, and build transparent Skywalks for visitors to crowd upon (this last attraction, cantilevered over thin air on the West Rim, is actually terrifyingly good fun; hualapaitourism.com). But what you really want when you're standing at the edge of Arizona's world-famous golden chasm is silence. And you're most likely to get it on the whispery North Rim (pictured), so head there for a crowd-free view — and more memorable moment. Beware, though: it's only accessible between May and October, due to winter snowfall.

Editor's tip: It's a long day, but you can combine the North and South Rims for an unforgettable dawn-to-dusk experience. Sleep over at Grand Canyon Lodge, North Rim (grandcanyonforever.com) to catch the sunrise, then drive 340km to the South and find that magical viewing spot for sunset.

Andalusia, Spain

They never found El Dorado, but 16th-century Spanish explorers came back from Peru with a different kind of gold. Today *los girasoles* (sunflowers) blanket 3,500sq km of Andalusian countryside in vivid yellow blooms from late May to June. They're at their most prolific on the sweltering plains around Seville, where the gigantic fields are seed- and oil-producing money-spinners — but to see them in a more splendid setting, drive south towards the historic clifftop city of Ronda, stopping off in Sierra de Grazalema Natural Park. Here, the sunny blooms merge with olive groves and whitewashed farmsteads to form a patchwork across the gnarled mountainsides.

Editor's tip: You can hop on a bike and ride through the park's less strenuous foothills, passing beneath swathes of gilded orbs — most beautiful come late afternoon (andalucia.com).

Pura Ulun Danu Bratan, Bali, Indonesia

Seemingly afloat and glowing like a boat of solid gold, this temple on Bali's Lake Bratan appears to defy physics. In fact, it's an optical illusion caused by heavy rain, as rising water levels make islands of this 17th-century Hindu-Buddhist temple complex — though against a backdrop of mist-cloaked mountains, it's a suitably magical setting for a sanctuary to the water goddess Dewi Danu. Arrive just before sunset, to see the temple blazing against the darkening sky, while the last of the day's light is cast across the lake in a kaleidoscopic slick of oranges, pinks and blues. And visit during the first week of July, to catch the dramatic end of the Bali Arts Festival, a month-long, rub-your-eyes riot of colour, costumes, theatre and cinema spread across capital Denpasar.

Editor's tip: Don't miss the buzzing Candikuning Market in nearby Bedugul, where you'll find pyramids of fruit — juicy mangosteens, tamarillos, tangerines and strawberries — piled implausibly high. The temple is 90 minutes from Denpasar and an easy day trip.

Ginza, Tokyo

The skulk down a side alley; the puzzled glance from map to defunct-looking office building; the tentative lift down to the basement... Finding a world-famous cocktail bar in Tokyo feels surprisingly dodgy. But Bar High Five is worth it, embodying the grit and giddiness of its affluent neighbourhood, Ginza, and found on a nocturnal safari through its streets — past girls in vertigo-inducing heels and peacocky frocks, faux-moonlight bouncing off the futuristic cubes that pass for designer stores. Your side-street skulk pays off as you exit the vandalised lift to a velvety, wood-panelled lounge, with a library-like wall of whiskies, sakes and more whimsical Japanese spirits. Don't expect a menu: the experts at this World's Best Bar contender will shake up something more bespoke. Then it's back into Ginza's human traffic, for another obscure mission to another unfathomable Tokyo address .

Editor's tip: Got limited time on the ground? Aim to fly in to Haneda Airport — it's a 20-minute drive into the city centre, rather than the hour it takes from Narita Airport.

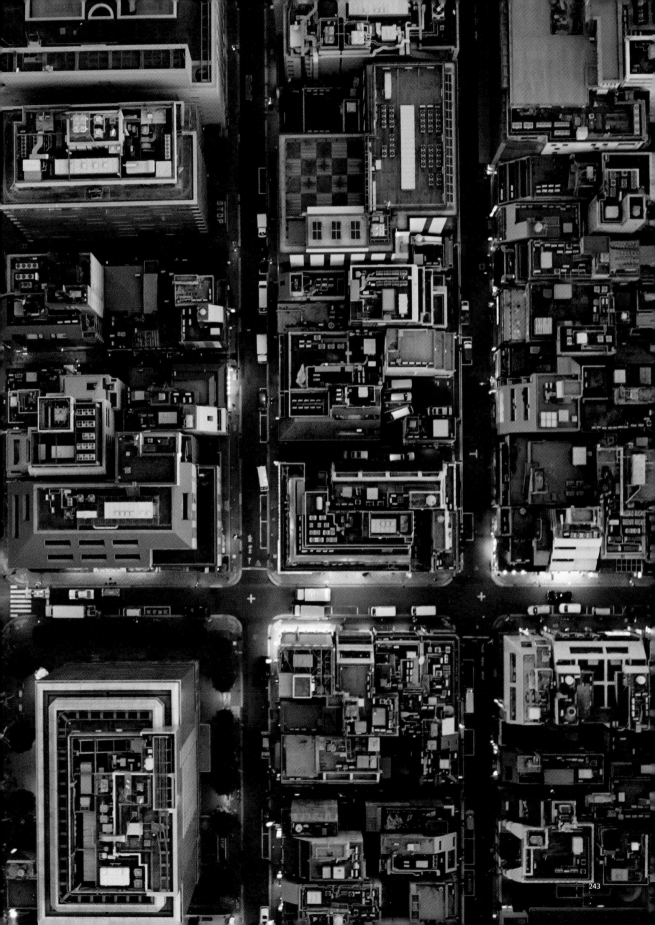

Acropolis, Greece

It's early in the morning, and the sun is already warming the terracotta-hued rooftops of the Greek capital. Your spine begins to tingle as you scale the Acropolis — the stone steps of this ancient citadel, first built on a rocky outcrop over Athens several millennia ago, have been polished smooth by the thousands of footsteps that have fallen before yours. At the pinnacle, the creamy columns of the Parthenon, the most iconic of the citadel's remaining temples, stand chiselled against technicolour-blue sky — sending those tingles into overdrive. Is that the whisper of Athena, the goddess of wisdom and war for whom the Parthenon was built, that you hear ringing out between the 2,500-year-old pillars? For a few moments, everything is still. Then, just before the chattering tour group pours in behind you, you make your exit via the *peripatos*, a hidden ancient path winding down the Acropolis' north slope —ensuring the magic isn't shattered.

Editor's tip: Skip the lengthy queue by pre-purchasing a multi-site pass at one of Athens' other big attractions (onodysseus. culture.gr), and get up there at the very start of the day.

Rajasthan, India

Perhaps it's no surprise that the inhabitants of Rajasthan, India's desert state, should be so drawn to colour. Visit the northwestern region and you'll soon notice that the people, their towns — and above all their jewellery and clothes — deliver a riotous rainbow of rebukes to the arid land. Jaipur, the pink city, and Jodhpur, the blue, stand alongside fabulous palaces and status-symbol forts built by the maharajahs. Their great patronage of local arts and handicrafts lingers on in the vivid markets and shops where you should throw yourself into the haggling spirit — India's shopping is at its finest here. Pick up some colourful bangles (if not the full 52 that married women wear up to their shoulders) as well as bags and bright textiles dyed and woven locally.

Editor's tip: Even animals get in on the act: in March, Jaipur's elephant festival sees the beasts dazzle with paint and ornaments; in October, at the Pushkar camel fair, farmers drape cattle with multicoloured pompoms and tassels.

Giza, Egypt

From a distance, they're super smooth, geometry-class cutouts set against a sun-drenched sky; alien spaceships touched down in an endless sea of sand. But journey closer, and the brute human muscle behind the pyramids begins to emerge — myriad hand-cut stone blocks, quarried, chiselled and lifted into place by 100,000 slave workers. Now, nearly 5,000 years after construction, the blocks' crisp edges have been softened, rounded by endless desert sandstorms, and centuries of grave-robbers and tourists. Arrive early to cheat the heat, and for the best chance of entering the dark passages within, with only the Pharaoh's ghosts for company.

Editor's tip: Beat the downtown Cairo traffic by taking a short metro ride to Giza, then joining a mini-van or bus there. Scams are rife, so avoid anyone who approaches you en route to the vehicles, and check in advance with your hotel how much you should pay for the transfer, agreeing the fare with your driver before boarding.

Washington DC, USA

Comfy shoes. They may not be what we picture smart, power-hungry Washingtonians wearing, but they're what you'll need for the hike around DC's sprawling sights. This hallowed political ground now feels more like a film set, thanks to the flurry of US government dramas on our TV screens — *House of Cards, Scandal, Madam Secretary* — not to mention the political circus watched worldwide since *that* election. Along with The White House and the ivory tusk of the Washington Monument, the Capitol Building, where the US Senate meets, should be top of your hitlist. Its three-tiered dome gleams brighter than ever, thanks to a 2016 polish, while its ornate, gilded Rotunda is exquisite.

Editor's tip: Capitol Building tickets are free, but should be bought in advance online (visitthecapitol.gov) — otherwise you'll need to queue first thing for limited same-day passes.

Orcia Valley, Tuscany, Italy

Tuscany has called to sun-starved Brits for generations — the poet Shelley called it a 'paradise of exiles' — and nowhere does Tuscany better than the Orcia Valley. Dotted with hilltop towns and vineyards, and carpeted with poppies in summer, the Valley, one hour south of Siena, is Tuscany at its cypress-studded best. Crisscrossed by olive-grove trails linking medieval villages, this is a walker's Promised Land, with the hilltop towns of Pienza, Radicofani, and Montepulciano the most exquisite stops for a cultural fix.

Editor's tip: The trick in Tuscany is not to overdo the big-name cities. Yes, Florence is a feast, and Siena is a stunner, but even unheralded Tuscan towns are staggeringly lovely — campari among the locals, for example, in the square at Sarteano is an authentic, tourist-free treat.

Buddha Park, Laos

You need to value artistry as much as antiquity to appreciate Buddha Park in Vientiane. On first sight, you'd swear its 200 ornate, moss-covered statues of Buddhist and Hindu deities were ancient. But in fact these huge religious casts were created from reinforced concrete by self-styled holy man Luang Pu between 1958 and 1975, so the oldest isn't even pensionable yet. Suspend your cynicism and the park's eccentricity will soon work its charm. The reclining Buddha pictured, with its soulful sweep, is the centrepiece, though the most memorable is the 'Pumpkin' — you can step inside this latter's gaping, demonic mouth, climb three floors representing Hell, Earth and Heaven, and emerge to showstopping views over the Mekong River.

Editor's tip: Most of the statues face east, so visit in the morning for photographs of the statues lit up by the rising sun.

Index

1
101 Tower 176

A
Aarhus 179
Abaco Islands 163
Abacos, The 163
Abraham Lake 202
Abu Dhabi 226
Accademia gallery 231
Acropolis 244
Adriatic Sea 59
Afghanistan 163
Africa 24, 35
Agra 31, 187
Aguas Calientes 101
Aït Benhaddou 225
Alamo Square 149
Alberta 202
Albi 175
Albuquerque 217
Albuquerque International
 Balloon Fiesta 217
Alexandros 130
Algar de Benagil 223
Algarve 223
Algiers 184
Alkmaar tulip fields 62
Alps 38, 113
Alpsee 38
Alsace 88
Amalfi Coast 35
Aman Resort 10
Amsterdam 50, 62
Amsterdam-Noord 50
Anaga mountains 31
Anatolian plateau 62
Andalusia 241
Andes 101, 126
Angkor Wat 49
Ang Thong 60
Annapurna 198
Annapurna Circuit 198
Antarctica 153
Antrim 55
Apia 94
Appenzell Alps 119
Arabian Sea 84, 117
Arc de Triomphe 69
Arctic 159, 228
Arctic Circle 141
Arctic Ocean 70
Argentina 113
Arizona 184, 239
Aros 179
Art Deco festival 192
Aswan 28
Athens 244

Atlantic Ocean 52, 64, 121, 189
Australia 22, 24, 123, 181, 192
Austria 132, 235
Aveiro 154
Avignon 144
Ayers Rock 123
Ayutthaya 60

B
Bacuit Bay 115
Bahamas, The 163
Bahía Magdalena 159
Baikal, Lake 97
Baja California 159
Bali 241
Bali Arts Festival 241
Bangkok 55, 60, 66
Bar High Five 242
Barbados 208
Barcelona 214
Basel 88
Bavaria 24, 38
Bazaruto Archipelago 156
Bedugul 241
Beijing 176, 233
Belfast 55
Belgium 137, 179
Belize 149
Benagil 223
Berlin 92
Bhutan 163, 192
Big Drop Off 40
Big Sur 50
Black Mountains 149
Black Rock Desert 166
Blanc, Lac 113
Blue Cypress Lake 230
Blue Harbour hotel 104
Blue Hole 149
Boa Vista 66
Bodiam Castle 125
Bognor Regis 76
Bogoria, Lake 69
Bolivia 126, 228
Bora Bora 237
Borneo 79
Borobudur 121
Bosnia 171
Botswana 24
Boudhanath Stupa 198
Brandenburg Gate 92
Bratan, Lake 241
Brazil 80, 121, 126
Brecon Beacons 149
Bremm 198
Brighton Pier 154
British Virgin Islands 79
Bromo, Mount 182
Bruges 179
Brussels 137

Buckingham Palace 180
Budapest 128
Buddha Park 250
Buenos Aires 113, 151
Bund, The 12
Bungle Bungles, The 24
Buñol 14
Burano 235
Burj Khalifa 36
Burning Man Festival 166
Burundi 28
Buttermere 76
Buza 59

C
Cairns 181
Cairo 246
Calabria 91
Calamari 218
Calderdale 18
California 50, 159
Camargue, The 210
Cambodia 49
Cambre Woods 137
Campement Zmela 35
Canada 202
Cancún 184
Candikuning Market 241
Cannaregio 169
Canouan 208
Canouan Resort 208
Cape Town 64
Cape Verde 66
Capitol Building 248
Capitol Hill (Seattle) 117
Capri 91, 142
Carenage Bay 208
Caribbean 14, 79, 136, 173,
 208
Carnival 19
Casa Batlló 214
Casa Mila 214
Casa Vicens 214
Castello district 169
Castellucio di Norcia 99
Catalonia 214
Ceará 121
Cenote Azul 197
Centraal Station
 (Amsterdam) 50
Chalet Robinson 137
Chamonix 113
Chamonix Needles 113
Charles Bridge 16
Charleston 205
Chefchaouen 88
Chicago 88
Chichén Itzá 184
Chichester 235
Chile 179, 220

China 12, 32, 99, 135, 146, 164,
 176, 213, 233
Chinatown 107
Chitwan National Park 198
Coimbra 132
Col des Montets 113
Colfax 104
Colorado river 184
Colosseum 206
Conegliano 223
Cook Islands, The 141
Copacabana 80, 121
Cornwall 117
Cortez, Sea of 159
Costa Rica 11
Coustellet 144
Creek, The (Dubai) 36
Croatia 59, 171
Cuba 122

D
Damaraland 52
Damaraland desert 191
Damnoen Saduak Floating
 Market 55
Damrak canal 50
Danube 128
Darjeeling 163
Dead Sea 188
Denmark 179, 213
Denpasar 241
Derwent Fells 76
Diamond Hill MTR station 57
Disney World 230
Ditchling Beacon 202
Ditchling Road 202
Divarata 130
Dos Ojos 197
Douz 35
Drake Passage 152
Dubai 36
Dubai Mall 36
Dubrovnik 59

E
East Africa 141, 156
East Sussex 125, 154
Easter Island 179
Egypt 28, 246
Eiffel Tower 69, 135
El Caminito 151
El Castillo 184
El Nido 115
El Pit 197
Empire State Building 94
Empty Quarter 192
England 18, 46, 180
Epcot 226
Espiritu Santo 99
Etosha 52

Etosha National Park 191
Everest 198
Excelsior Crater 163

F
Faroe Islands 213
Ferdinand-Hanusch-Platz 132
Figueira da Foz 154
Fiji 99
Financial District
  (San Francisco) 149
Finland 141
Fiordland National Park 177
Firefly hotel 104
Flégère 113
Florence 231, 248
Flores 44
Florida 226, 230
Fly Geyser 166
Fogo 66
Folly Island 205
Four Mile Beach 181
France 88, 113, 144, 175, 210
Frégate Island 213
French Polynesia 237
Frolikha Adventure Coastline
  Track 97
Fuji, Mount 158
Fushimi Inari Taisha 218

G
Galata Bridge 161
Gam Gam 169
Gam Gam Goodies 169
Ganesh Visarjan Festival 117
Garbara 223
Geiranger 206
Geiranger Fjord 206
Gelarto Rosa 128
Georgia 32
Germany 38, 92, 198
Giant's Causeway 55
Ginza 242
Giza 246
Gobbins, The 55
Golden Horn 161
Golden Lion pub 117
Gracia district 214
Grand Canal 169
Grand Canyon 184, 239
Grand Canyon Lodge 239
Grand Mosque 226
Grand Place 137
Great Abaco 163
Great Barrier Reef 181
Great Jaguar Temple 44
Great Lakes, The 97
Great Rift Valley 37
Great Wall 233
Greece 82, 91, 150, 218, 244

Green Cay 79
Green Park 180
Grenada 136
Groeningemuseum 179
Gros Islet 14
Grote Markt 179
Guanabara Bay 80
Guangxi Province 213
Guatemala 44
Guilin 213
Guilin province 164

H
Hagia Sophia 161
Haigh-Ashbury district 149
Halifax 18
Halnaker 235
Halnaker Hill 235
Haneda Airport 242
Hang En Cave 139
Hangzhou 99
Hanoi 139
Harbin Snow and Ice
  Festival 146
Harbour View Hotel 200
Harris, Isle of 173
Havana 122
Havasu Creek 184
Havasu Falls 184
Hawaii 62
Hawkdun Range 49
Hay Bluff 149
Hebden Bridge 18
Hebrides 173
Herberg Vlissinghe 179
Hierapolis 62
High Atlas Mountains 225
Himalayas, The 163
Hohensalzburg Fortress
  132
Hoher Kasten 119
Holi Festival 31
Hong Kong 57, 176
Hope Town 163
Hualapai Hilltop 184
Huangpu river 12
Hungary 128
Hyde Park 180

I
Iceland 144, 189, 213
Idaburn Dam 49
Idaho 104
Ij 50
Île aux Aigrettes 103
Inari, Mount 218
India 31, 84, 163, 173, 187,
  198, 245
Indian Ocean 58, 64
Indonesia 121, 182, 241

Inle Lake 108
Interstate 405 20
Inverness 173
Ipanema 80
Ischial 142
Island Camp 69
Israel 188, 192
Istanbul 161
Italy 35, 91, 99, 142, 144, 169,
  184, 223, 231, 248
Izmailovsky Market 43

J
Jaipur 173, 245
Jamaica 104
James Bond Beach 104
Japan 87, 158, 218
Java 121, 182
Jemma el Fna 165
Jerónimos monastery 132
Jinshanling 233
Jodhpur 245
Jordan 40, 192
Junkanoo Summer
  Festival 163

K
Kaikoura 177
Kakku Pagodas 108
Kangchenjunga, Mount
  163
Kandy 202
Kapitelplatz 132
Karlova street 16
Kata Tjuta 123
Katelijnestraat 179
Kathmandu 198
Kathmandu Valley 198
Kaua'i 62
Kefallonia 130
Kenya 37, 69, 141
Kerala 84
Keswick 76
Keukenhof tulip fields 72
Keyhole Arch 50
Khao Phing Kan 26
Kiev 126
Kimberleys, The 24
King Henry's Mound 46
Kirkjufell 189
Klevan 126
Kobe 87
Koblenz 198
Koningsdag festival 72
Konstanz 119
Kowloon 57
Kruger park 191
Kuala Lumpur 32
Kuşadasi 62
Kyoto 218

L
La Barrica cafe 151
La Boca 151
La Bombonera 151
La Paz 228
La Pedrera 214
La Tomatina 14
Laamu Atoll 223
Ladakh 163
Lake District 76
Landwasser Viaduct 74
Laos 250
Las Fallas Festival 74
Las Teresitas 31
Leaf Beach 223
Les Praz 113
Les Routes de la Lavande 144
Levera Beach 136
Li, River 213
Lighthouse Inlet 205
Lion's Head Mountain 64
Lion Pavillion 57
Lion Rock 57
Lion Rock Country Park 57
Lisbon 132
Little India (Singapore) 107
Little Tibet 163
Logar Valley 235
London 36, 46, 180, 235
Londonderry 55
Longsheng 164
Los Angeles 20
Luganville 99
Luskentyre Sands 173
Luxor 28

M
Machu Picchu 101
MacLehose Trail 57
Madagascar 111
Magnificent Mile 88
Mahébourg 103
Malabar Coast 84
Malaysia 32
Maldives, The 58, 156, 223
Malé 223
Manhattan 94, 194
Manhattan Beach 20
Manneken Pis fountain 137
Manohara hotel 121
Marche 99
Marina Bay Sands hotel 107
Marina Corricella 142
Marrakech 88, 165, 225
Masai Mara 141
Matterhorn 74
Mauritius 103
Mayan Riviera 197
Mediterranean Sea 88, 184, 210
Mekong River 251

Melanesia 99
Mer de Glace 113
Mexico 159, 184, 197
Miami 126
Midway Geyser Basin 163
Milford Sound 177
Millennium Park 88
Milsons Point 200
Mission District 149
Mont Blanc 113
Mont Blanc, Massif du 113
Montenegro 10
Montepulciano 248
Monti Sibillini National
  Park 99
Monument Valley 8
Moon Hill 135
Morocco 88, 165, 225
Morondava 111
Morris Island Lighthouse 205
Moscow 43
Mosel River 198
Mosel Wine Route 198
Mozambique 156
Mozartplatz 132
Mulhouse 88
Mumbai 117
Munich 24, 38
Musée de la Lavande 144
Myanmar 108
Myrtos Beach 130

N
Namib Desert 52
Namibia 52, 191
Namolokama 62
Napier 192
Naples 142
Narita Airport 242
Naseby 49
Nassau 163
Natural Reserve of São
  Jacinto 154
Navagio Beach 150
Navajo Nation
  Reservation 8
Nepal 163, 198
Netherlands 62, 72
Neuschwanstein Castle 38
Nevada 166
New Mexico 217
New York 94, 194
New Zealand 49, 94,
  177, 192
Newquay Station 117
Nile, The 28
Niterói 80
North Island (New Zealand) 192
North Pole 70
North Rim 239

Northern Ireland 55
Northern Lights 189
Norway 70, 206

O
OCBC Skyway 107
Ocean Drive 126
Ocho Rios 104
Odek plywood factory 126
Okavango 24
Oktoberfest 24
Old Arbat Street 43
Old Town (Prague) 16
Olgas, The 123
Olhuveli Island 223
Oman 192
One World Observatory 94
Oracabessa 104
Orcia Valley 248
Oregon 104
Ormesini canal 169
Oruro Carnival 126

P
Pacific Ocean 40, 50, 159, 179
Palau 40
Palawan Island 115
Palazzo Vecchio 231
Palermo 113, 184
Palheiros da Tocha 154
Palouse 104
Palouse Hills 104
Pamukkale 62
Papara 50
Paris 69, 135
Park Güell 214
Paro Taktsang 192
Parque de María Luisa 196
Parthenon 244
Patagonia 220
Patisserie Academie 179
Pearl Tower 12
Pehoé, Lake 220
Penanjakan, Mount 182
Peripatos 244
Perl 198
Peru 101, 241
Petra 40
Phang Nga Bay 26
Philippines 115
Phong Nha-Ke Bang National
  Park 139
Piazza San Marco 169
Pienza 248
Pike Place Fish Market 117
Pine Box bar 117
Piton Mountains 14
Playa del Carmen 197
Plaza de España 196
Plaza del Ayuntamiento 74

Plitvice Lakes National
  Park 171
Pointe d'Esny 103
Polynesia 141
Ponta Grossa 121
Ponta Grossa village 121
Port Douglas 181
Port Gaverne 117
Port Isaac 117
Port Quin 117
Port Quin Bay 117
Porto 154
Porto train station 132
Portofino 91
Portugal 132, 154, 223
Positano 35
Prague 16
Praia da Concha 154
Praia da Marinha 223
Procida 142
Prosecco Road 223
Provence 144, 210
Pub Royal 202
Pudeto 220
Puerto Natales 220
Puget Sound 117
Pura Ulun Danu Bratan 241
Pushkar camel fair 245
Pyhä Lake 141
Pyramids 246
Pyrenees 210
Pyrgos 82

Q
Queen's Hotel 202
Queensland 22
Queenstown 49, 177
Quintana Roo 197
Quiraing 35

R
Radicofani 248
Raffles hotel 107
Ragusa 184
Rainier, Mount 117
Rajasthan 173, 245
Ranthambore 173
Ranthambore National
  Park 173
Rarotonga 141
Ras-el-Maa 88
Ravello 35
Refugio Paine Grande 220
Reykjavík 144, 189
Rhône 210
Richmond Park 46
Rift mountains 88
Rift Valley 37, 69
Rinka Falls 235

Rio de Janeiro 19, 80, 121,
  126, 163
Rio Grande 217
Ripponden village 18
Riquewihr 88
Riri Blue Hole 99
Rivoire 231
Rome 206
Ronda 241
Route 1 (Iceland) 144
Rue Charles Buls 137
Russia 43, 83, 97
Ryburn Valley 18

S
Sagrada Família 214
Sahara 31, 35
Sahara, Festival of the 35
Sainte-Marie, Île 111
St George 184
St James's Park 180
St Lucia 14
St Mary 104
St Moritz 74
St Paul's Cathedral 46
St Petersburg 83
St Stephen's Basilica 128
St Vincent and the
  Grenadines 208
Sal 66
Salar de Uyuni 228
Salzburg 132
Salzburg Festival 132
Sambódromo 19
Samburu National Park 37
Samoa 94
San Andrés 31
San Francisco 149
San Salvatore castle 223
San Telmo 113
Sandia Mountains 217
Sandy Spit 79
Santa Croce 169
Santa Cruz 31
Santiago (Cape Verde) 66
Santo Antao 66
Santorini 82
São Filipe 66
Sarteano 248
Saudi Arabia 192
Savannah 32
Saviour on Blood, Church
  of the 83
Scandinavia 141
Scotland 173, 213
Seattle 117
Seljalandsfoss 144
Senegal 66
Sepilok 79
Serengeti National Park 141

Serpentine Gallery 180
Serpentine Lake 180
Seventy Islands 40
Seville 196, 241
Seychelles 213
Sha Tin Pass Road 57
Shanghai 12, 99
Shard, The 36
Shark City 40
Shibden House 18
Shibden Valley 18
Shipwreck Beach 150
Shisr 192
Shizuoka province 158
Siberia 97, 146
Sicily 184
Siem Reap 49
Siena 248
Sierra de Grazalema Natural
  Park 241
Silver Lake 20
Singapore 107
Skeleton Coast 191
Skydeck, The Ledge at 88
Skye, Isle of 35
Slindon 235
Slovenia 235
Snæfellsnes Peninsula 189
Solna Centrum 102
Songkran Water Festival 66
Sossusvlei 52
South Africa 64, 191
South Beach 126
South Carolina 205
South Downs 202, 235
South Island (New Zealand)
  49, 177
South Pacific 94, 99, 141
South Rim 239
South West Coast path 117
Southern Bus Terminal
  (Bangkok) 55
Southern Ocean 152
Space Needle 117
Spaceship Earth 226
Spain 14, 74, 196, 210, 214,
  241
Sri Lanka 202
Stane Street 235
Steakhouse 113
Steiner Street 149
Steptoe Butte 104
Steptoe Butte State
  Park 104
Stockholm 102
Stokkseyri 144
Strasbourg 88
Sumatra 79
Sumhuram 192
Sun Island 228

Supai 184
Svalbard 70
Sveti Stefan 10
Sweden 102
Swiss Alps 74
Switzerland 88, 119
Sydney Harbour
  Bridge 200
Sydney Opera
  House 200
Széchenyi Baths 128
Szimpla Kert, The 128

T
Ta Prohm 49
Table Mountain 64
Tahiti 50
Taipei 176
Taiwan 176
Taj Mahal 31, 187
Tamba 87
Tanzania 141
Tapati Rapa Nui Festival 179
Taransay 173
Tarn river 175
Taverna 218
Teahupoo 50
Temple IV (Chichén Itzá) 44
Temple of the Sacred
  Tooth 202
Temple V (Chichén Itzá) 44
Tenerife 31
Thailand 26, 60, 66
The Glacier Express 74
Thean Hou 32
Theresienwiese
  fairground 24
Tibet 198
Tibetan plateau 163
Tijuca National Park 80
Tikal 44
Tikal National Park 44
Titicaca, Lake 228
To-Sua Ocean Trench 94
Tokyo 218, 242
Torres del Paine National
  Park 220
Tortuguero 11
Tower of Pisa 205
Trattoria al Gatto Nero 235
Treasury, The 40
Treviso 223
Tulum 197
Tunis 184
Tunisia 35
Tunnel of Love 126
Turkey 62, 161
Turquoise Coast 62
Turquoise Pool 163
Tuscany 248

Tutira, Lake 192
Two Mile Reef 156
Tyrrhenian Sea 35

U
Ukraine 126
Uluru 123
Umbria 99
United Arab Emirates
  36, 226
United Kingdom 125, 154,
  173, 202, 235
Upolu 94
Upper Paro Valley 192
Urban Food Market 192
United States of America
  8, 20, 32, 50, 88, 104,
  117, 149, 163, 166, 184,
  205, 217, 226, 230, 239,
  248
Utah 8
Uttar Pradesh 31

V
Vágar Island 213
Vailima 94
Valdobbiadene 223
Valencia 14, 74
Valladolid 184
Valley of the Wind 123
Vanuatu 99
Venice 169, 223, 235
Venice Beach 20
Via Garíbaldi 169
Victoria 213
Victoria Harbour 57
Victoria Peak 57
Victory Column 92
Vientiane 251
Vietnam 139
Viewpoint One 182
Viewpoint Two 182
Villa Rufolo 35
Villa Sandi 223
Vlamingstraat 179
Vltava, River 16

W
W Trek 220
Waikopiro, Lake 192
Wales 149
Walt Disney World 226
Washington (state) 104
Washington DC 248
Washington Monument,
  The 248
Wat Muang 60
West Bank 188
West Lake 99
West Rim 239

West Street 135
West Sussex 235
Western Ghats 84
Western Princeville Ocean
  Resort, The 62
White House, The 248
Whitehaven Beach 22
Whitsunday Islands 22
Whitsunday Passage 22
Wight, Isle of 154
Willis Tower 88
Windamere Hotel 163
Windermere 76
Wolwedans Dune Camp 52
Wong Tai Sin 57
World Showcase 226
Wormsloe Plantation 32
Wye Valley 149
Wyoming 163

Y
Yangshuo 135, 213
Yao Noi 26
Yellowstone National
  Park 163
Yellowstone River 163
Yemen 192
Yogyakarta 121
Yotsutsuji 218
Yucatán Peninsula 184
Yugoslavia 10

Z
Zaanse Schans 72
Zakynthos 150
Zermatt 74
Zürich 119

Image Credits